Service Quality

FOUNDATIONS FOR ORGANIZATIONAL SCIENCE
A Sage Publications Series
Series Editor
David Whetten, *Brigham Young University*
Editors
Anne S. Huff, *University of Colorado* and *Cranfield University* (UK)
Benjamin Schneider, *University of Maryland*
M. Susan Taylor, *University of Maryland*

The FOUNDATIONS FOR ORGANIZATIONAL SCIENCE series supports the development of students, faculty, and prospective organizational science professionals through the publication of texts authored by leading organizational scientists. Each volume provides a highly personal, hands-on introduction to a core topic or theory and challenges the reader to explore promising avenues for future theory development and empirical application.

Books in This Series

PUBLISHING IN THE ORGANIZATIONAL SCIENCES, 2nd Edition
Edited by L. L. Cummings and Peter J. Frost

SENSEMAKING IN ORGANIZATIONS
Karl E. Weick

INSTITUTIONS AND ORGANIZATIONS
W. Richard Scott

RHYTHMS OF ACADEMIC LIFE
Peter J. Frost and M. Susan Taylor

RESEARCHERS HOOKED ON TEACHING:
Noted Scholars Discuss the Synergies of Teaching and Research
Rae André, and Peter J. Frost

THE PSYCHOLOGY OF DECISION MAKING: People in Organizations
Lee Roy Beach

ORGANIZATIONAL JUSTICE AND HUMAN RESOURCE MANAGEMENT
Robert Folger and Russell Cropanzano

RECRUITING EMPLOYEES: Individual and Organizational Perspectives
Alison E. Barber

ATTITUDES IN AND AROUND ORGANIZATIONS
Arthur P. Brief

IDENTITY IN ORGANIZATIONS: Building Theory Through Conversations
Edited by David Whetten and Paul Godfrey

PERSONNEL SELECTION: A Theoretical Approach
Neal Schmitt and David Chan

BUILDING STRATEGY FROM THE MIDDLE: Reconceptualizing Strategy Process
Steven W. Floyd and Bill Wooldridge

MISSING ORGANIZATIONAL LINKAGES: Tools for Cross-Level Research
Paul S. Goodman

THE CONTINGENCY THEORY OF ORGANIZATIONS
Lex Donaldson

ORGANIZATIONAL STRESS: A Review and Critique of Theory, Research, and Applications
Cary L. Cooper, Philip J. Dewe, and Michael P. O'Driscoll

INSTITUTIONS AND ORGANIZATIONS, Second Edition
W. Richard Scott

ORGANIZATIONAL CULTURE: Mapping the Terrain
Joanne Martin

PERSONALITY IN WORK ORGANIZATIONS
Lawrence R. James and Michelle D. Mazerolle

CAREERS IN AND OUT OF ORGANIZATIONS
Douglas T. Hall

ORGANIZATION CHANGE: Theory and Practice
W. Warner Burke

COMPENSATION: Theory, Evidence, and Strategic Implication
Barry Gerhart and Sara L. Rynes

SERVICE QUALITY: Research Perspectives
Benjamin Schneider and Susan S. White

Benjamin Schneider
University of Maryland and Personnel Research Associates, Inc.

Susan S. White
Personnel Decisions Research Institutes, Inc.

Service Quality
Research Perspectives

Foundations for
Organizational
Science
A Sage Publications Series

SAGE Publications
International Educational and Professional Publisher
Thousand Oaks ▪ London ▪ New Delhi

For information:

Sage Publications, Inc.
2455 Teller Road
Thousand Oaks, California 91320
E-mail: order@sagepub.com

Sage Publications Ltd.
6 Bonhill Street
London EC2A 4PU
United Kingdom

Sage Publications India Pvt. Ltd.
B-42, Panchsheel Enclave
Post Box 4109
New Delhi 110 017   India

Printed in the United States of America

Library of Congress Cataloging-in-Publication Data

Schneider, Benjamin, 1938-
Service quality: Research perspectives / Benjamin Schneider,
Susan S. White.
    p. cm. — (Foundations for organizational science)
Includes bibliographical references and index.
ISBN 0-7619-2146-X (Cloth) — ISBN 0-7619-2147-8 (Pbk.)
    1. Customer services—Quality control—Research. 2. Customer
services—Management—Research. 3. Consumer satisfaction—Research. I. White,
Susan S. II. Title. III. Series.
HF5415.5.S338 2004
658.8′12—dc21   2003014201

This book is printed on acid-free paper.

03   04   05   06   07   10   9   8   7   6   5   4   3   2   1

Acquisitions Editor:	Al Bruckner
Editorial Assistant:	MaryAnn Vail
Production Editor:	Diane S. Foster
Copy Editor:	Stacey Shimizu
Typesetter:	C&M Digitals (P) Ltd.
Proofreader:	Olivia Weber
Indexer:	Molly Hall
Cover Designer:	Michelle Lee Kenny

Contents

List of Tables

List of Figures

For Boaz, Chloe, Cipora, Gabriel, and Gillian . . . and their futures.

Poppy

For Mike, Mom, and Dad.

Susan

Introduction to the Series

The title of this series, *Foundations for Organizational Science (FOS)*, denotes a distinctive focus. FOS books are educational aids for mastering the core theories, essential tools, and emerging perspectives that constitute the field of organizational science (broadly conceived to include organizational behavior, organizational theory, human resource management, and business strategy). Our ambitious goal is to assemble the "essential library" for members of our professional community.

The vision for the series emerged from conversations with several colleagues, including Peter Frost, Anne Huff, Rick Mowday, Benjamin Schneider, Susan Taylor, and Andy Van de Ven. A number of common interests emerged from these sympathetic encounters, including enhancing the quality of doctoral education by providing broader access to the master teachers in our field, "bottling" the experience and insights of some of the founding scholars in our field before they retire, and providing professional development opportunities for colleagues seeking to broaden their understanding of the rapidly expanding subfields within organizational science.

Our unique learning objectives are reflected in an unusual set of instructions to FOS authors. They are encouraged to (a) "write the way they teach," framing their books as extensions of their teaching notes rather than as expansions of handbook chapters; (b) pass on their "craft knowledge" to the next generation of scholars, making them wiser, not just smarter; (c) share with their "virtual students and colleagues" the insider tips and best bets for research that are normally reserved for one-on-one mentoring sessions; and (d) make the complexity of their subject matter comprehensible to nonexperts so that readers can share their puzzlement, fascination, and intrigue.

We are proud of the group of highly qualified authors who have embraced the unique educational perspective of our *Foundations* series. We encourage your suggestions for how these books can better satisfy your learning needs—as a newcomer to the field preparing for prelims or developing a dissertation proposal or as an established scholar seeking to broaden your knowledge and proficiency.

—David A. Whetten
Series Editor

Acknowledgments

We want to thank very much the reviewers who provided such valuable comments on this manuscript. These include Susan Jackson (who wrote us long, thoughtful notes), Matt Sobel (whose comments appropriately sometimes began "No, No, No" over something we wrote), David Whetten (who is clearly a conceptual thinker you want on your side), and Kiane Goudarzi (whose insights on services marketing were so useful). In addition, we want to thank the editors of the *Foundations for Organizational Science* series for encouraging us to tackle this project. Finally, we want to thank Marquita Fleming, the former editor at Sage for the FOS series, for her enthusiasm and expressions of interest in us doing this book.

1 Introducing Service Quality

Desert your online customers and they'll return the favor. . . . For ten tips on how to enhance the customer service experience at your site, visit www.liveperson. com/tips or call us at 1.877.228.7984.

— LivePerson, 2000

Customer loyalty is won or lost by how you manage all the ways your customers interact with your company. . . . To see how you can provide a more positive customer experience every time, visit www.genesyslab.com or call 1.888.GENESYS.

— Genesys, 2000

Calls for businesses to pay attention to the quality of the service they deliver their customers have grown increasingly loud over the past few decades, even before there were the service delivery issues connected to the Internet—with its get-your-book (Amazon.com), find-your-future (Monster.com), and lose-your-savings (e-trade.com) Web sites. Scholars may not always be at the cutting edge of business, but in the late 1970s researchers in a variety of disciplines and in a number of countries began to produce a now-substantial body of theory and research devoted to understanding service quality. Scholars from all walks of the academic world—marketing, operations management, human resources management, organizational behavior, industrial and organizational psychology, consumer behavior, and sociology—have made contributions to understanding what service is, how service and service delivery quality are experienced by customers, and the role of the employee and his or her organization in service delivery.

On the one hand, the topic of service quality seems fairly straightforward and simple—everyone knows it when they experience it. Certainly, everyone has a favorite service-quality story, and it is usually about how bad service can be! But the idea that studying service quality is an easy endeavor ignores the complexities that lie beyond surface-level glances at the topic. In actuality, even such basic issues as defining the dimensions of service delivery and service quality have been the subject of intense academic—and, in many cases, business—debate. And this is all before we get to the issue of how to create and deliver service that will be experienced by customers in positive ways.

The purpose of this book is to present a sense of these debates and reveal some of the intriguing intricacies that surround the conceptualization and assessment of issues that bound the topic of service quality. In this introductory chapter, we first discuss the philosophy that guided our approach for the present book. Then we address several questions: (a) Why did the field of service quality emerge? (b) What are services? and (c) Why is service quality an important topic to study? Finally, we conclude the chapter with an overview of the topics covered in the remainder of the book.

Approach of the Book

What the Book Is Not

First, let us say what this book is *not*. This is not a textbook. That is, we make no claims at covering all of the relevant research literature on service delivery, let alone on service quality. Fine texts on service quality now exist that do a wonderfully complete job of showing what we know and how what we know is being used (see, for example, Lovelock, 2001; Zeithaml & Bitner, 2000). This is also not a book written for managers seeking actions they can take to make immediate improvements in the service they deliver to customers. Here, too, excellent books exist (see Berry, 1999; Lovelock, 1994). Of course, the manager concerned with alternative ways of thinking about service quality, and/or looking at some research findings as a basis for decisions that must be made, could find this book interesting for the ways it discusses service quality.

If you are tired of searching for nuggets in a case-method approach to education, this book may help you by presenting alternate lenses for viewing service quality issues. Thus this is not a book designed to be used in case-driven MBA classes on service quality (cf. Sasser, Hart, & Heskett, 1991). While some approaches to research are presented in detail, we also pay a lot of attention to how to think about service from a variety of perspectives. It is this thinking that could prove useful, especially to managers who find themselves charged with service quality management in a firm.

What the Book Is

Having addressed what the book is not, let us turn to what the book is. The book is primarily for students interested in research and theory about service quality. We focus specifically on the quality of service delivery, paying less attention to the service product or the core service—the food in the restaurant or the clothes in the department store. In addition, we focus very heavily on consumer services—banks, department stores, hotels—rather than on services that require less interaction with customers—electricity generation, for example. Finally, our focus on consumer services leads us pretty much to ignore professional services, such as legal and medical services, where the professional requirements for entering into the delivery of such services are stringent and governed by state law.

Our approach is to discuss in some detail selected streams of thinking and research on the delivery of consumer services from a variety of disciplines, including marketing, organizational studies (including industrial-organizational psychology, organizational behavior, and human resources management), and operations management. We have selected these streams based on the impact they appear to have had on the broad field of services management, and we attempt to reveal how thinking has evolved about service quality and service delivery in each of these areas in the past 25 years. Not a bad deal for such a slim volume!

Several goals prompted our approach to this book. One goal was to reveal how scholars from different academic backgrounds and perspectives approach and conduct research on service delivery. How do they think about service delivery? What are the key questions they address? How do they carry out their empirical research? What have they learned? A second goal was to explicate a framework or model of service delivery that simultaneously incorporates internal organizational functioning and the external user or customer. Business firms, after all, exist not only for the benefits of the members of the firm, but also for the people the firm serves. For too long, the internal world of the organization has been seen by organizational scholars as separate or distinct from the external world it serves. Furthermore, those who have been concerned with the external customer have paid less attention than they might to internal organizational functioning—though it must be said that services marketing researchers have been more concerned with the internal organization than organizational scholars have been concerned with the external customer. We hope to show organizational scholars in particular how these worlds are conceptually and empirically linked.

Thus our primary audience is researchers in organizational studies— organizational behavior (OB), human resources management (HRM), and industrial and organizational psychology (I-O). This audience was chosen by us because (a) we are organizational studies people ourselves, of the I-O persuasion; (b) organizational studies has not paid sufficient attention to the external customer and the thinking and research surrounding customer experiences that has characterized services marketing; and (c) organizational studies has not paid sufficient attention to the operational issues associated with service delivery, such as the design of service facilities and the importance of the presence of customers when services are produced and delivered. Our long-term goal in introducing these marketing and operational theories and research to organizational scholars is to enhance the conceptual and practical relevance of research in the fields that focus on organizational functioning and organizational behavior.

There is much theory and research we will not review. As noted earlier, we have decided to be selective and review a few streams of thinking and research in some detail rather than attempt to be encyclopedic. Our hope is that readers of this volume will come away with the same kind of enthusiasm we have for trying to understand the complex and interlocking issues raised by the topic of service quality. We need new ideas to keep pushing the frontiers of our understanding of service delivery forward (Lovelock, 2001; Schneider, 2001). We hope the messages we send through this book will generate such new ideas, new approaches, and new progress. Let's begin by seeing how we got where we are.

What Are Services?

A major reason for the development of the field now called services marketing and management was the realization that services were—in the extreme—different from goods. We typically think of a service as something that is done for us or to us. We get the car repaired, we go to the doctor, or we go to the bank. But this way of thinking about service provides little insight into what really makes a service a service. If services are no different from goods, for example, then everything we know about goods and product quality should apply. But services are different in some very interesting ways, beginning with the distinction between what the service product is—the food, the clothing—and what service delivery is. In what follows, we first consider this issue in some detail and then discuss three continua along which services and goods can be distinguished: intangibility, simultaneous production and consumption, and heterogeneity.

Technical vs. Functional Outcomes

A brief discussion of the terms *services* and *service quality* is in order. More specifically, there is typically a *how* and a *what* component to services. That which is delivered is the *what* of service delivery (e.g., the meal eaten in a restaurant). The *how* of service concerns the service delivery process itself (e.g., the processes involved in being seated, in ordering the meal, the meal being brought to the table and served, the attention accorded the patrons while they consume the meal). Grönroos (1990) distinguished these two aspects of service from each other, calling the former a *technical outcome* dimension of service and the latter a process-related or *functional* dimension of service.

While both technical and functional outcomes are important contributors to total service quality perceptions, the process or delivery aspect of service delivery has been the focus of most service quality literature in services marketing and management. Therefore, when services and service quality are discussed, the terms almost always refer to service delivery. Of course, this is not to say that the functional dimension (i.e., delivery) is more important than the technical outcome. When having surgery, the technical competence of the doctor is probably more important to most people than his or her bedside manner. However, when dining out, people often pay large premiums for the delivery aspect of the experience. Thus the relative importance of the technical and functional components of services will vary but this will not be our concern here.

We will now turn to certain defining characteristics of services, noting that these are most applicable to the functional/delivery component. These characteristics are intangibility, inseparability, and heterogeneity. As will be discussed, the three characteristics described below can all be considered continua on which different types of services will vary. It should also be noted that these three characteristics are not the only way of defining services. In fact, we will present other definitions in later chapters. Different definitions are useful for different purposes, and our intent is not so much to integrate them as to present particular definitions for illustrating particular points. To begin, the definitions presented below are useful for highlighting differences between services and goods.

Defining Characteristics of Services

Relative Intangibility. Most important, services in the extreme are deeds, processes, and performances (Zeithaml & Bitner, 2000). Shostack (1987) states it this way:

> Services are not things. McLuhan (1964) perhaps put it best and most succinctly more than 20 years ago when he declared that the *process* is the product. We say "airline" when we mean "air transportation." We say "movie" when we mean "entertainment services." We say "hotel" when we mean "lodging rental." The use of nouns obscures the fundamental nature of services, which are processes not objects. (p. 34)

A defining characteristic of a pure service is intangibility. That is, pure services cannot be seen, touched, held, or stored—they have no physical manifestation. Purchasing a pure service does not result in anything that can be packaged and put in a bag to take home. Rather, because of their intangibility, pure services are essentially processes that are experiences: "Services yield psychological experiences more than they yield physical possessions" (Schneider & Bowen, 1995, p. 19).

Our favorite examples of pure services are entertainment experiences: listening to and watching a symphony orchestra playing Beethoven or actors in a Shakespeare play. These services, when personally experienced in the theater, are defined by the musicians' or actors' processes; they have no tangible attributes that can be taken home, shown to others at a later point in time, or literally touched. They are, in a word, intangible. The intangibility of the experience is made especially salient by thinking about how an evening at the symphony compares to buying a physical recording of a symphony playing a particular piece. While the music itself can be captured on a CD, the experience of attending a concert cannot.

Of course, not all services are "pure services," and many have tangible components. That is, services are not all intangible, but rather are arrayed on a continuum of intangibility. When people go to a restaurant to eat, they purchase both a physical meal (tangible component) as well as the delivery of the meal (intangible component). Furthermore, many physical goods also have an intangible service component to them. Personal computer manufacturers not only must manufacture their tangible computers, but also must market their computers to customers, provide warranty support and maintenance for their products, and so forth.

In sum, many products are made up of both tangible goods and intangible delivery experiences. At the extremes are pure services that have no tangible component and pure goods that have no intangible component. However, most fall between the two extremes of the intangibility continuum, having both tangible and intangible elements. Accordingly, virtually every organization should be concerned with issues of service quality and service delivery. How consumers evaluate intangible service delivery is explored in detail in Chapter 2, where we examine the services marketing research that has been accomplished on the measurement of service quality.

Relative Inseparability. Pure services, which are composed entirely of a delivery experience, cannot be produced at one time and place and then stored for later use at another place. Thus pure services, like Beethoven concerts and Shakespeare plays, are produced by organizations and consumed by customers at the same time. In the pure case, the processes of production and consumption cannot be separated. The inability to produce services before they are consumed means that there is no way to produce a service, check it for defects, and then deliver it to a customer—the production and consumption occur simultaneously. Take the symphony orchestra. When the conductor brings down the baton, production and consumption are inseparable—they occur together. Given this inseparability, it is obvious that no quality-control checks can be done between production and consumption and that the production cannot be saved for someone to hear at another time in another concert hall (unless, of course, it is recorded for such use).

A very interesting feature about the inseparability of services is that organizations must strive to ensure that, when the service is produced, the maximum number of people are available to consume it. United Airlines, for example, will fly flight number 288 from Denver to Washington, D.C., only once on May 30. Any seat not filled will never exist again; it cannot be inventoried for later use. Is it any wonder

United Airlines has so many different tactics, from frequent flyer miles to a vast array of ticket prices, for filling seats?[1] Or, consider the Montgomery, Alabama, Embassy Suites Hotel: On June 21, 2004, it will have 125 rooms to fill and any room unfilled that date can never be recovered. Embassy Suites must obviously do everything it can, including offering a free night at the hotel if there is any dissatisfaction whatsoever, to fill those beds.

In fact, the field of operations management has developed several models, falling under the rubric *yield management* (also known as "revenue management") for dealing with these kinds of issues. We will have more to say about these models in Chapter 3, when we discuss the operation of service delivery firms.

Relative Heterogeneity. Services also differ from physical goods in that services are relatively more heterogeneous than goods in their production and their delivery. Services production and delivery frequently involve the interaction of both service personnel and customers, and the human element in this production and delivery process can result in no two service instances being identical. Thus different customers might have different demands that need to be met, or different service personnel might go about meeting the same customer demands somewhat differently at different points in time. For example, one customer might enter a bank wanting to make a deposit, while another wants to make a withdrawal; one is in a hurry and the other is passing the time of day; one has several accounts with large balances and the other only uses his or her account for cashing checks. Each of these bank customers is availing him- or herself of "bank services," but they present different sets of demands, expectations, and desires, and the service delivery staff must continually adapt to these differences. Moreover, even the same demand might be satisfied differently depending on the people involved. One teller might be new to the bank and unable to process the withdrawal without assistance from another teller, while another teller might process the transaction with no assistance at all. The point is that service production and delivery, due to the frequently interactional nature of production and delivery, is less standardized than the production of goods. This relative heterogeneity can make services more difficult to measure and to do quality-control checks ahead of time to ensure that they meet uniform standards. Rather, service production and delivery, because of the human interaction they frequently involve, are heterogeneous.

Some of the implications of heterogeneity for the management of the internal organization will be addressed in Chapters 3 and 4. In Chapter 3, the focus will be on the application of operations management principles in the face of the inherent variability introduced into service firms by the presence and participation of customers. In Chapter 4, the interaction of employees and customers across the firm-customer boundary will be of particular interest.

Summary. Intangibility, inseparability, and heterogeneity all obviously range from high to low. The higher on the continua, the more like a pure service it is; the lower on the continua, the more like a pure good it is. What we want the reader to begin to feel are some of the differences between services and goods that these continua elaborate so that we can jointly adopt a "service production and delivery logic" rather than a "manufacturing goods logic" when it comes to thinking about service quality. In the remainder of the book, we will frequently speak of "service" and "services" as if they all exist on the extremes of the continua we have described. This will be shorthand for us to connote the idea that we are focusing on the service end of the continua while we simultaneously understand that many services accompany goods, just as many goods have accompanying services. It must be emphasized that both manufactured goods and service products contribute to the quality experience, but we are here concerned primarily with the service delivery process—what Grönroos (1990) called "functional quality" (compared to the technical quality of the good or service product itself). How to define *quality* is the next issue of interest.

What Is Quality?

Now that we have discussed what we mean by *services*, we will turn to a discussion of what we mean by *quality*. While defining quality may seem easy at first glance, it is difficult to establish a single, universal definition for it. "Quality is an ambiguous term. On the one hand, everyone knows (or thinks they know) what quality is. On the other hand, formulating a comprehensive and uniform definition is a big—if not insurmountable—problem" (Kasper, van Helsdingen, de Vries, 1999, p. 184). As described below, there are several different ways to approach the definition of quality: the philosophical approach, the technical approach, and the user-based approach.

Philosophical Approach

First, there is a philosophical approach to quality (Kasper et al., 1999; Oliver, 1997). This perspective holds that quality is synonymous with *innate excellence* (e.g., attainment of superiority, achieving desirability, or becoming useful; Oliver, 1997, p. 166) and that it cannot be defined or analyzed further than that. Under this approach, people know quality when they see it, but they cannot define quality further (sounds like the definition of pornography to us!). While this view of quality might have its supporters, it is useless from either a research or practice perspective to consider quality as unknowable and unmeasurable.

Technical Approach

The second approach to defining quality is in stark contrast to the first, and considers quality from an objective and absolute perspective. Alternatively called *manufacturing-based quality, objective quality,* or *conformance quality,* this approach to quality is concerned with the extent to which a product conforms to technical standards (Kasper et al., 1999; Oliver, 1997). In this approach, quality is often measured objectively in terms of number of deviations from these standards or number of defects (e.g., a "zero-defect" policy). Because this approach to quality is so focused on the objective and the readily measurable, it is very well suited to measuring the quality of standardized products that are mass-produced.

User-Based Approach—The Focus of the Present Book

The third approach to defining quality is the user-based one, in which the quality of a product is determined by its user. This definition of quality takes the view that quality is subjective and hinges on the individual perceptions of customers. The quality of a product is high when customers say it is—and this is not always when the product conforms to technical criteria. This user-based view toward quality has been particularly appealing in trying to define quality in the realm of services.

The user-based view of quality is attractive for service quality because of the nature of service delivery. First, the increased intangibility of service delivery means in the extreme that people cannot physically touch services, but can only perceive them in their minds. Thus measuring the quality of service delivery as perceptions of the user is particularly appropriate for assessing the quality of services. Furthermore, since a defining feature of services is their heterogeneity across time and people, an approach to quality that reflects this variability in service delivery is essential for defining service quality.

Of course, it is possible to measure service quality with more objective criteria, as in the technical approach to quality. Services could be compared to a checklist of quality indicators, such as whether calls are answered in three rings or whether employees remember to smile and say "thank you" to customers at least 99% of the time. However, setting specific goals for particular aspects of service might narrow the vision of employees so that they will achieve those goals by lowering quality in areas for which no goals have been set. For example, service representatives might start answering all customer calls within three rings by terminating other customer calls or placing people on hold. This situation would not be an overall improvement in service quality, even though the objective, technical approach to quality might indicate that it was. Thus a user-based approach, rather than an objective checklist approach, has been found to be superior for evaluating the quality of intangible services.

In sum, the features of service delivery match a subjective, user-based approach to quality considerably better than they match an objective, technical approach. The user-based perspective has therefore become the main approach to assessing quality in the services literature. Of course, the more objective approaches to measuring quality still have their place for measuring the technical outcomes of service experiences (e.g., the meals themselves, whether the car now runs properly). The technical approaches are more appropriate for measuring the quality of the *what* of services, while the user-based approaches are more appropriate for measuring the quality of the *how*. Furthermore, because the central focus of marketing theory is customers, defining quality in user terms has led marketing scholars to dominate the area of service quality research. This is a clear-cut deviation from the association of technical approaches to quality with the field of operations management (Kasper et al., 1999).

Why Is the Study of Service Quality Important?

The Emergence of the Service Quality Field

It cannot be taken for granted that service quality is a topic worthy of study. In fact, the field of quality control was around for decades before service quality began to be viewed as a separate domain. Before moving on, we will briefly describe how the field of service quality emerged.

The push for organizations to pay serious attention to issues of quality is certainly not new. As early as the 1920s, statistical processes for quality control were being developed at Bell Laboratories by Walter Shewhart. Over time, these processes were developed and refined, and were implemented during World War II to control the production of war materials in factories throughout the United States. However, despite these developments, there was no widespread "quality movement" in this country until several decades later.

The same was not the case in Japan. In the 1940s and 1950s, two Americans, W. E. Deming and J. M. Juran, started teaching Japanese companies methods for controlling the quality of the goods that they produced. These teachings relied heavily on monitoring errors in production and finding ways to minimize them. That is, the ultimate goal of the quality movement introduced in Japan was to eliminate variation in the quality of products produced. Efforts to do this focused primarily on adjusting and improving the systems used to manufacture goods; improving quality meant improving the design and manufacturing process for products— with the result being a consistently high-quality product. Based on these principles, an entire field of quality control developed in Japan.

At the same time, however, the United States was not focusing its attention on these types of quality controls. Indeed, as noted earlier, Deming and Juran left America for Japan to find an audience more receptive to their ideas than the one they found in the United States. With the post–World War II boom in demand for production that U. S. companies experienced, quality controls were simply not of overriding importance. "After the war, companies were too busy to bother [with quality]. Swamped by pent-up demand, they cranked out products and let quality fend for itself" (Port & Carey, 1991, p. 10). Thus while Japanese companies were trying hard to reduce variability in the products at the time of production, U.S. companies tended to adopt the approach of fixing mistakes after they happened. Consequently, U.S. companies were devoting a large amount of labor (and therefore money) to the process of reworking defective items. They were operating under the model that there is always time to fix something, but never enough time to do it right the first time.

Beginning in the early 1970s, however, U.S. companies were forced to reevaluate their approaches to manufacturing. Increased global competition threatened the survival of many U.S. companies, and drove home the point that change, especially change in the way product quality was viewed, was necessary. Looking to their Japanese rivals for ideas on becoming more competitive, many U.S. companies tried to copy what was happening in Japan. For example, with mixed success, many workplaces implemented quality circles—groups of employees gathered to discuss ways of improving quality on the shop floor—in their efforts to improve manufacturing processes and reduce errors in production (Adam, 1991; Cole, 1979). In addition, many companies, such as AT&T, Xerox, Ford, and ITT, applied the work of Genichi Taguchi and his quality engineering system. As Taguchi (1993) noted,

> Simply put, the purpose of quality engineering is to conduct the research necessary to develop robust technologies and methods that increase the competitiveness of new products by reducing their cost and improving their quality; this enables the manufacturing enterprise to survive in the highly competitive global market. (p. 5)

Thus the need to recapture competitiveness vis-à-vis foreign rivals brought quality issues to the forefront in many U.S. companies.

The quality movement in U.S. manufacturing is still alive and well—although we typically hear of it only when the winner of the Malcolm Baldridge Award is announced. In 1987, the Malcolm Baldridge National Quality Award Improvement Act established a set of evolving criteria that would serve as the basis for winning the award, with companies self-nominating into the competition. Applying for the award is a lengthy process, and companies literally spend years preparing themselves for the competition. Winners of the award have included Motorola, IBM, Ritz-Carlton, and 3M, among others. (See Spechler, 1993, for an interesting introduction to the Baldridge Award and companies who have successfully competed for it.)

Product quality in the United States is no longer big news because, although it has taken almost a quarter century of effort, U.S. manufacturing production is now world-competitive in terms of quality. The Baldridge Award competition is partially responsible, in that winners of the award are required to make their processes and procedures public, thereby serving as an example and model to others. The advent of reengineering in the 1990s (Hammer & Champy, 1993) has also been effective in pushing along the quality emphasis, with the technology revolution making statistical quality-control processes available directly on the shop floor. Information technology at every level of the manufacturing process allows information to be automatically captured so that quality can be monitored as production occurs. Because of this data-rich environment, we now have just-in-time manufacturing and the flexibility required to adapt to momentary needs for increased or decreased levels of production for specific products. The models and processes for these options existed in the early 1950s, but the technology to make such information immediately available on the shop floor did not. Now we have both. This new world of technology has obviously had a tremendous impact on production and production quality. But what has been the effect on service quality and service delivery?

Statistical quality-control processes were developed almost exclusively for testing and measuring products for the presence of defects. These principles do not apply easily to the topic of service delivery. More specifically, the intangibility of service delivery, its simultaneous production and consumption, and the natural requirements for heterogeneity (variance) in the delivery of services (see Zeithaml & Bitner, 2000) make it difficult to apply the statistical quality-control models to services delivery. Nevertheless, there has more recently been some excellent work on application of quality-control logic to service production. We detail this work in Chapter 3.

How Big Is the World of Service, Anyway?

An important factor in the growth of academic and practical interest in service quality has been the growth of service industries, especially in western countries. The development of new models of quality geared toward services has become increasingly important as services have come to dominate the economies of many western countries. As Zeithaml and Bitner (2000) note, "Services marketing concepts and strategies have developed in response to the tremendous growth of services industries resulting in their increased importance to the U.S. and world economies" (pp. 5–6). Statistics compiled by the U.S. Bureau of Economic Analysis shed light on the trend of increased services growth and are summarized in Table 1.1. This table presents a percentage breakdown of the U.S. gross domestic product (GDP) by types of industry.

The category of "Services" includes hotels and other lodging places; personal services; business services; auto repair, services, and parking; miscellaneous repair services; motion pictures; amusement and other

Table 1.1 Percentage Breakdown of U.S. Gross Domestic Product (GDP) by Industry

	% of GDP				
	1959	*1967*	*1977*	*1987*	*1997*
Private Services-Producing Industries (Total)	**48.8**	**49.8**	**51.9**	**59.1**	**63.9**
Transportation and Public Utilities	80.9	80.5	80.9	90.0	80.3
Wholesale Trade	70.1	60.9	70.0	60.4	60.9
Retail Trade	90.7	90.4	90.4	90.3	80.8
Finance, Insurance, and Real Estate	13.6	14.1	14.0	17.7	19.4
Services	90.5	10.9	12.6	16.7	20.4
Private Goods-Producing Industries (Total)	**38.9**	**36.0**	**32.8**	**27.3**	**24.2**
Agriculture, Forestry, and Fishing	40.0	30.0	20.7	10.9	10.6
Mining	20.5	10.8	20.7	10.9	10.5
Construction	40.7	40.7	40.6	40.6	40.1
Manufacturing	27.7	26.5	22.8	18.9	17.0
Government	**12.8**	**14.1**	**14.5**	**13.9**	**12.7**

SOURCE: Yuskavage (1996) for data through 1987; Lum and Moyer (1998) for 1997 data.

NOTE: The categorization of industries as *service-producing* or *goods-producing* follows the scheme employed by the Survey of Current Business (published by the Bureau of Economic Analysis). Accordingly, the category of *services* includes hotels and other lodging places; personal services; business services; auto repair, services, and parking; miscellaneous repair services; motion pictures; amusement and other recreation services; health services; legal services; educational services; social services; membership organizations; miscellaneous professional services; other services; and private households.

recreation services; health services; legal services; educational services; social services; membership organizations; miscellaneous professional services; other services; and private households. A review of Table 1.1 illustrates the dominant role that services have come to play in the U.S. economy. It also indicates that this role has been a substantial one for some time. Even in 1959, services-producing industries represented a larger fraction of the U.S. GDP than did goods-producing industries.

The gap between the two has continued to widen since that time, with services representing a larger and larger share of the GDP and goods representing a smaller and smaller one. The contrast between the growth trends of services and goods is particularly apparent when the percentage of GDP due to manufacturing is compared to that due to services. In 1959, manufacturing accounted for 27.7% of the GDP, while services accounted for only 9.5%. That is, the manufacturing component of the economy was almost three times as large as the services component. However, by 1987, the advantage of manufacturing over services was less than 2 percentage points, and services had surpassed manufacturing by 1997. It should also be noted that this services growth trend is not unique to the United States. In 1988, services made up more than half of the GDPs of South Africa, Egypt, Mexico, Japan, Brazil, Spain, Canada, the United Kingdom, France, and Australia as well (Zeithaml & Bitner, 2000).

The larger role assumed by service industries in the U.S. economy over time is also reflected in the breakdown of labor-force statistics. In 1959, approximately 38% of nonagricultural, private sector employees worked for goods-producing industries, while 62% worked for services-producing ones. However, by 1997, these numbers had shifted to 20% and 80%, respectively (Bureau of Labor Statistics, 2000).[2] Thus over three fourths of the private sector (nonagricultural) labor force is currently employed by services-producing industries.

In sum, service quality developed as a field separate from manufacturing quality in the late 1970s and early 1980s. Quality had been advocated as a weapon that companies could use to survive fierce global competition, but different models from those created for the manufacturing world needed to be developed for controlling the quality of service delivery. The differences between services and goods made the objective, technical methods of controlling quality for goods difficult to apply to intangible, heterogeneous service delivery in the world of consumer services. Thus the service quality literature was developed. Furthermore, this literature has grown and gained in importance as services have become a larger part of western economies.

The Appropriate Focus on Profits

So service is a large component of the economy. But why should any one company be interested in improving its service quality? In the previous section, we referred to service quality as a tactic that companies could adopt to gain a competitive advantage over others. Here, we will address this issue further. We will attempt to answer the question of why the study of service quality is important by focusing on the benefits to organizations of delivering high-quality service.

As with virtually all organizational endeavors, the arguments made in support of the quality movement are tied to profits. The quotations that we presented at the beginning of the chapter are testament to the pervasive thought that offering quality service can have financial payoffs for a company. While the relationship is not perfect, there is growing support for a link between an organization's emphasis on service quality and profitability (Deshpandé, Farley, & Webster, 1993; Narver & Slater, 1990; Schneider, 1991). This idea is captured in the *service profit chain*, a theoretical framework developed by the Service Management Interest Group at the Harvard Business School (Heskett, Sasser, & Schlesinger, 1997). One representation of the service profit chain incorporates the links shown in Figure 1.1.

Internal Functioning of the Organization. The service profit chain depicted in Figure 1.1 focuses first on the internal functioning of the organization—what goes on within the organization in terms of the design of the workplace and its employees that allows the organization to function and to meet the demands of its customers. Starting the service profit chain with internal organizational functioning emphasizes the point that the delivery of quality service does not simply happen on its own. Rather, efforts must be made to facilitate employees in their efforts to deliver quality service.

In other words, employees must receive the necessary tools and resources to deliver quality service. They must receive adequate resources and training, have the equipment and supplies required for their work, and have the supportive managerial practices and assistance they need (Burke, Rapinski, Dunlap, & Davison, 1996; Schneider & Bowen, 1985, 1993; Schneider, White, & Paul, 1998). As Reynoso and Moores (1995) point out, "If management wants its employees to deliver an outstanding level of service to customers, then it must be prepared to do a great job with its employees" (p. 65). Furthermore, employees must receive good service from others within the organization in order to deliver good service to external customers (Grönroos, 1990; Reynoso & Moores, 1995).[3]

However, while work facilitation and internal service are both necessary for the delivery of external service quality, they are not sufficient.

18

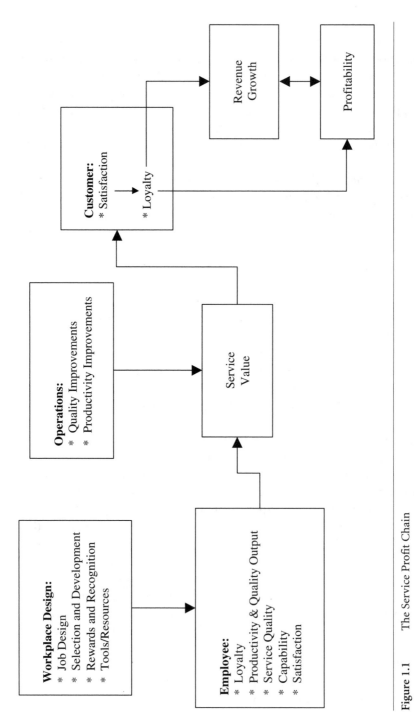

Figure 1.1   The Service Profit Chain

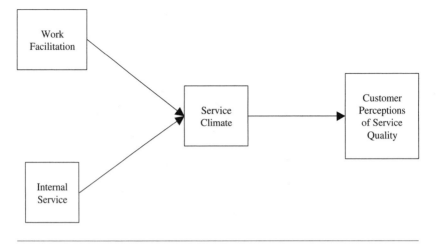

Figure 1.2   Relationships Among Internal Functioning Variables and Service Quality

SOURCE: From Schneider et al. (1998). Copyright ©1998 by American Psychological Association. Used with permission.

Rather, they have been discussed as a foundation for an organization's climate for service (Schneider et al., 1998). An organization's climate for service has been defined as its employees' perceptions about the extent to which they are expected to delivery quality service, and the extent to which they are supported in and rewarded for their efforts to deliver quality service (Schneider, 1990; Schneider et al., 1998). The relationships between internal service, work facilitation, and climate for service have been represented as follows in Figure 1.2. (Note that this model was designed with external customers in mind, and most empirical tests of these types of relationships also rely on perceptions of external customers. However, the logic applies even to internal end-user customers.)

When an organization has a strong climate for service, its policies, practices, and procedures will reflect the importance of service to the organization, and its employees will believe that the organization values service quality. For example, an organization with a strong service climate would formally evaluate its employees on their delivery of quality service, and it might also base a portion of employees' compensation on such evaluations. These sorts of procedures would send the message to employees that service quality is important to the organization.

Several empirical studies have supported the link between the internal functioning of an organization (i.e., climate for service and internal service) and the level of quality delivered to external customers. Beginning with a seminal article in 1980, Schneider and his colleagues demonstrated that the way employees perceived their organization's service climate was related to the way that customers perceived the service that they received (Schneider, Parkington, & Buxton, 1980). This relationship has since been replicated a number of times by a number of different researchers (Hartline & Ferrell, 1993; Johnson, 1996; Schmit & Allscheid, 1995; Schneider & Bowen, 1985; Schneider et al., 1998; Wiley, 1991). The research linking internal functioning and customer perceptions will be discussed in greater depth in Chapter 4.

External Service. What happens on the inside of an organization has been shown to relate to the quality of service customers report receiving. In turn, the latter part of the service profit chain deals with the consequences of delivering quality service to external customers. Specifically, it ties service quality to desirable organizational outcomes, such as customer satisfaction and loyalty, which ultimately lead to profits. In other words, the service chain depicted in Figure 1.1 illustrates the idea that when customers receive quality service, they will be satisfied with the organization providing the service. Their satisfaction with the organization will in turn lead them to be loyal customers to the organization, repeatedly purchasing the service in question from the organization. Finally, the repeat business of loyal customers translates into higher profits.

These ideas have been well captured in an approach to demonstrating the effects of service quality developed by Rust, Zahorik, and Keiningham (1994, 1996) labeled *return on quality* (ROQ). They view service quality as an investment that organizations make that should generate a positive return. Like the service profit chain diagrammed in Figure 1.1, this approach also holds that service improvements should lead to increased customer satisfaction, which in turn should lead to beneficial behavioral intentions on the part of customers. These might include the intention to return to the organization or to recommend the organization to a friend. Next in the sequence, these intentions translate into actual behaviors, and these behaviors lead to financial benefits, such as increased revenues and profits. The approach of Rust et al. (1994, 1996) will be discussed further in Chapter 3.

From an empirical viewpoint, several studies provide support for the link between service quality and behaviors that are indicative of customer loyalty. For example, Boulding, Kalra, Staelin, and Zeithaml (1993) found a positive relationship between customers' perceptions of overall service quality and their intentions to exhibit loyalty and positive word-of-mouth behaviors (i.e., making recommendations to others). In addition, Rust and Zahorik (1993) found relationships between customers' perceptions of the service they received and customer retention. The researchers found that satisfaction with the factor of "warmth" (composed of such scales as "friendliness" and "employees listen to my needs") was the strongest predictor of retention in their sample of bank customers. White and Schneider (2000) also found that customers with higher perceptions of service quality were more likely to remain customers of organizations and to tell other people about their experiences. These and other studies indicate that service quality can impact customer commitment and behaviors.

The relationship between loyalty and profits essentially occurs through two paths: increasing revenues and decreasing costs. First, loyal customers generate a steady stream of revenues for the company by repeatedly making purchases from it. In other words, rather than switching from company to company to buy a service, loyal customers return to the same organization repeatedly. In addition, loyal customers can serve as valuable marketing tools for organizations by telling their friends and families that they too should become customers of the organization in question (Christopher, Payne, & Ballantyne, 1991; Dick & Basu, 1994; Furlong, 1993). By convincing others that they should switch organizations, loyal customers can essentially drum up new business and increase revenues for a service company. Christopher et al. (1991) have called these customers "advocates" of the organization.

Furthermore, it can be cheaper for organizations to serve repeat customers than new ones, thereby linking customer loyalty to profits via reduced costs (Christopher et al., 1991; Rust & Zahorik, 1993). Repeat customers can be easier to serve because the rules of the relationship have been defined; the participating members know each other and their respective roles and obligations (Congram, 1991). Furthermore, current customers are a potential base for cross-selling and are also a valuable source of new ideas for business strategies (Congram, 1991).

Because of the benefits of customer loyalty for increasing profits, recent writings have focused on the benefits to organizations of establishing long-term relationships with customers. This field has become known as *relationship marketing*. With relationship marketing, organizations try to form long-term alliances with customers by using "a combination of customized products, customized communication, and customized service and delivery—in effect, treating each customer as a unique segment of one" (Winkleman, Schultz, Edelman, & Silverstein, 1993, p. 29). Relationship marketing techniques are designed to make customers feel less like "numbers" and more like valued individuals whose needs are recognized and fulfilled by the organization. Examples of how this is done range from relatively minor acts on the part of the organization, such as addressing customers by name, to more substantial programs, such as giving current customers advance information on new products or sales (Brierly, 1994) and adding value to the credit cards of card holders (Gill, 1991).

Service Quality Is Only One Way to Profits

There is nothing wrong with making a profit, but there are lots of ways to make a profit without focusing on service quality. For example, innovation of product is one way to make a profit—just look at the pharmaceutical industry. Price is another tactic companies can use to make a profit. By selling at a lower price than anyone else, you can attract a certain kind of customer and make a profit—just look at Wal-Mart. Different strategies yield different business models in any industry. Consider the Marriott Corporation, with its Courtyards by Marriott, its Residence Inns, its Renaissance Hotels, and its Ritz-Carltons (among others)—all part of the Marriott Corporation, but run under different business models, focusing on different segments of the market place! Effective businesses define market segments whose needs they wish to meet and then pursue the tactics they feel best meet the segments' needs in what has been called the "focus or falter" model (Davidow & Uttal, 1989). The focus-or-falter model preaches that companies must make decisions about their market and then pursue that market with precision and dedication.

The service quality tactic is particularly interesting to us, because it requires a total systems view of how businesses operate. In the total systems view, all components of the service production and delivery process are important and all come into play simultaneously when a customer visits a service facility—from the nature of the internal organization to the nature of the organization's customers, to the relationship between customers and employees, to the physical space in which customers are served, to the tactics used for moving customers in and through the service delivery facility. We find it interesting to explore how to conceptualize and study these simultaneously functioning components of the service firm, and it is all the better if the conceptualization and the research show relationships to profits!

Summary

The economies of many western societies have undergone serious transformations with regard to where people work—from manufacturing to service—and the proportion of the GDP attributable to service industries. In this introductory chapter, we have laid the foundation for the remaining chapters by briefly reviewing the attributes of service and the implications of those attributes for service production and consumption, the history of the development of interest in quality, and the importance of service quality for revenues and profits in service organizations. Finally, we hinted at how interesting the study of service quality is as a total systems construct, one that requires attention from many vantage points. As a further introduction to these issues, we next outline the chapters in the remainder of the book.

Overview of the Rest of the Book

In the following chapters, we will progress through a series of topics related to service quality. We will begin by addressing one of the basic topics of the field: How is service quality defined and measured from the customers' vantage point? Answering this question has been the focus of marketing research, which concentrates on those who receive services—the customers. In subsequent chapters, we will move on to describing the "internal world" of service facilities and how they function to deliver the service customers experience. We will examine the internal functioning of organizations from two perspectives. In Chapter 3, the perspective will be from the vantage point of systems and processes for the production and delivery of services. In Chapter 4, the vantage point will shift to the employees and the OB/HRM systems in which they work as they deliver service to customers. The following section provides greater detail on the remaining chapters of the book.

Chapter 2 is devoted to a retail consumer-marketing perspective on service quality. That is, we focus on service quality from the customer's point of view. Our primary aim in the chapter is to trace the evolution of the definition and measurement of service quality as perceived by customers, focusing on the research program of Parasuraman, Zeithaml, and Berry and their development of the SERVQUAL model of service quality. The discussion of the SERVQUAL model, including criticisms that have been levied against it, will serve as a basis of comparison and backdrop for a discussion of alternative ways of defining, and therefore measuring, service quality (Parasuraman, Berry, & Zeithaml, 1991; Parasuraman, Zeithaml, & Berry, 1985, 1988, 1994a, 1994b; Zeithaml, Parasuraman, & Berry, 1990). The discussion will highlight several methodological issues, such as the use of focus groups in services research, the development of survey measures of (customer) attitudes, factor analysis, and validation.

Chapter 3 will focus on an operations management (OM) approach toward studying service. The key focus of OM is the effectiveness and efficiency of flows: flows of people, documents, and information into, through, and out of organizations. OM is about the design of processes in organizations to meet the parameters of interest, and one of those parameters is quality. As such, OM is the home of organizational quality improvement attempts, such as reengineering and process redesign and control (Hammer & Champy, 1993). In Chapter 3, we will describe some of the issues challenging those who have applied an OM approach to service delivery (e.g., the problem posed for quality when the customer is present in the service operation).

The fourth chapter in the book will focus on organizational climate and the climate for service. Again, these issues were briefly mentioned in this introductory chapter, but a much more in-depth picture of these topics will be painted in Chapter 4. This chapter begins with a history of the organizational climate construct and discusses the ways in which organizational imperatives are communicated to employees. We then move into a more detailed discussion focused on service climate in particular. We explore the organizational policies and practices that research and theory suggest actually create a service climate (i.e., what elements of organizational functioning should you focus on if you want to create and/or change a service climate?).

Chapter 5, the final chapter of the book, is dedicated to demonstrating how all facets of organizational functioning come together in a total systems perspective on the experiences of consumers. Consumers do not often care why or how a service emerges well or poorly. Consumers are judges of the outcome of organizational activity; everything organizations do vis-à-vis customers—marketing, OM, HRM/OB, and even the physical attributes of the settings in which service is delivered—has an impact on the service quality experiences customers have. We will show in this chapter how the HRM/OB literature has avoided issues of service delivery, service quality, and customers and note ways by which the introduction of these issues into HRM/OB might stimulate both conceptually interesting and practically useful research. The chapter indeed concludes with explicit research agendas that we feel should be accomplished to (a) introduce the customer and service into organizational studies, (b) introduce valuable lessons from OM and marketing into HRM/OB thinking and research, and (c) elevate the whole field of service quality research and thinking.

Notes

1. Obviously, United Airlines could use a smaller plane if one were available, but it is certainly more difficult to locate an extra plane than it is to price seats differentially to fill the scheduled plane.

2. The complete table may be viewed at www.bls.gov/webapps/legacy/cesbtab1.htm.

3. The idea of internal service is reflective of the idea that everyone is a customer—including coworkers, supervisors, and so forth. In fact, many support employees of organizations never even see an external customer, and exist only to provide service to others internal to the organization. The importance of internal service is becoming even more apparent with such trends as allowing employees to choose external sources for services provided internally if they can get them cheaper and/or at a better quality outside. Thus internal units may need to fight for their survival within the organization, and delivering quality service to their internal customers is one tool they can use.

References

Adam, E. E. (1991). Quality circle performance. *Journal of Management, 17*(1), 25–39.

Berry, L. (1999). *Discovering the soul of service: The nine drivers of sustainable business success.* New York: Free Press.

Boulding, W., Kalra, A., Staelin, R., & Zeithaml, V. (1993). A dynamic process model of service quality: From expectations to behavioral intentions. *Journal of Marketing Research, 30,* 7–27.

Brierly, H. (1994). The art of relationship management. *Direct Marketing, 57*(1), 25–26.

Bureau of Labor Statistics. (2000). Employees on nonfarm payrolls by industry sector and selected industry detail [Table]. Retrieved on June 30, 2003, from http://www.bls.gov/webapps/legacy/cesbtab1.htm.

Burke, M., Rapinski, M., Dunlap, W., & Davison, H. (1996). Do situational variables act as substantive causes of relationships between individual difference variables? Two large-scale tests of common cause models. *Personnel Psychology, 49,* 573–598.

Christopher, M., Payne, A., & Ballantyne, D. (1991). *Relationship marketing: Bringing quality, customer service and marketing together.* London: Butterworth-Heinemann Ltd.

Cole, R. E. (1979, November). Made in Japan: Quality-control circles. *Across the Board,* pp. 72–78.

Congram, C. (1991). Building relationships that last. In C. Congram (Ed.), *The AMA handbook of marketing for the service industries* (pp. 263–380). New York: AMACOM.

Davidow, W. H., & Uttal, B. (1989). Service companies: Focus or falter. *Harvard Business Review,* 69, 77–85.

Deshpandé, R., Farley, J., & Webster, F. (1993). Corporate culture, customer orientation, and innovativeness in Japanese firms: A quadrad analysis. *Journal of Marketing, 57,* 23–27.

Dick, A., & Basu, K. (1994). Customer loyalty: Toward an integrated conceptual framework. *Journal of the Academy of Marketing Science, 22*(2), 99–113.

Furlong, C. (1993). *Marketing for keeps.* New York: John Wiley.

Genesys. (2000, January 10). [Advertisement]. *BusinessWeek,* p. 49.

Gill, P. (1991). Added value: Relationship marketing is one way for retailers to build loyalty. *Stores, 73*(10), 39–40.

Grönroos, C. (1990). Relationship approach to marketing in service contexts: The marketing and organizational behavior interface. *Journal of Business Research, 20,* 3–11.

Hammer, M., & Champy, J. (1993). *Reengineering the corporation: A manifesto for business revolution.* New York: Harper Business.

Hartline, M., & Ferrell, O. (1993). *Contact employees: Relationships among workplace fairness, job satisfaction, and prosocial service behaviors* [Technical Working Paper]. Cambridge, MA: Marketing Science Institute.

Heskett, J. L., Sasser, W. E., Jr., & Schlesinger, L. A. (1997). *The service profit chain: How leading companies link profit and growth to loyalty, satisfaction, and value.* New York: Free Press.

Johnson, J. (1996). Linking employee perceptions to customer satisfaction. *Personnel Psychology, 49,* 831–852.

Kasper, H., van Helsdingen, P., & de Vries, W., Jr. (1999). *Services marketing and management: An international perspective.* Chichester, England: Wiley.

LivePerson. (2000, February 7). [Advertisement]. *Business Week,* p. EB 63.

Lovelock, C. H. (1994). *Product plus.* New York: McGraw-Hill.

Lovelock, C. H. (2001). *Services marketing: People, technology, strategy* (4th ed.). Englewood Cliffs, NJ: Prentice-Hall.

Lum, S., & Moyer, B. C. (1998, November). Gross product by industry, 1995–97. *Survey of Current Business,* pp. 20–40.

McLuhan, M. (1964). *Understanding media.* New York: McGraw-Hill.

Narver, J., & Slater, S. (1990). The effect of a market orientation on business profitability. *Journal of Marketing, 54,* 1–18.

Oliver, R. (1997). *Satisfaction: A behavioral perspective on the consumer.* New York: McGraw-Hill.

Parasuraman, A., Berry, L., & Zeithaml, V. (1991). Refinement and reassessment of the SERVQUAL scale. *Journal of Retailing, 67*(4), 420–450.

Parasuraman, A., Zeithaml, V., & Berry, L. (1985). A conceptual model of service quality and some implications for future research. *Journal of Marketing, 49*(4), 41–50.

Parasuraman, A., Zeithaml, V., & Berry, L. (1988). SERVQUAL: A multiple-item scale for measuring consumer perceptions of service quality. *Journal of Retailing, 64*(1), 12–40.

Parasuraman, A., Zeithaml, V., & Berry, L. (1994a). Alternative scales for measuring service quality: A comparative assessment based on psychometric and diagnostic criteria. *Journal of Retailing, 70*(3), 201–230.

Parasuraman, A., Zeithaml, V., & Berry, L. (1994b). Reassessment of expectations as a comparison standard in measuring service quality: Implications for further research. *Journal of Marketing, 58,* 111–124.

Port, O., & Carey, J. (1991, October 25). Questing for the best. *BusinessWeek,* pp. 8–16.

Reynoso, J., & Moores, B. (1995). Towards the measurement of internal service quality. *International Journal of Service Industry Management, 6,* 64–83.

Rust, R., & Zahorik, A. (1993). Customer satisfaction, customer retention, and market share. *Journal of Retailing, 69*(2), 193–215.

Rust, R., Zahorik, A., & Keiningham, T. (1994). *Return on quality: Measuring the financial impact of your company's quest for quality.* Chicago, Illinois: Probus.

Rust, R., Zahorik, A., & Keiningham, T. (1996). Return on quality (ROQ): Making service quality financially accountable. In R. Rust, A. Zahorik, & T. Keiningham (Eds.), *Readings in service marketing* (pp. 193–216). New York: HarperCollins.

Sasser, W. E., Jr., Hart, C. L. W., & Heskett, J. L. (Eds.). (1991). *The service management course: Cases and readings.* New York: Free Press.

Schmit, M. J., & Allscheid, S. P. (1995). Employee attitudes and customer satisfaction: Making theoretical and empirical connections. *Personnel Psychology, 48,* 521–536.

Schneider, B. (1990). The climate for service: An application of the climate construct. In B. Schneider (Ed.), *Organizational climate and culture* (pp. 383–412). San Francisco: Jossey-Bass.

Schneider, B. (1991). Service quality and profits: Can you have your cake and eat it, too? *Human Resources Planning, 14*(2), 151–157.

Schneider, B. (2001). Benjamin Schneider. In R. P. Fisk, S. J. Grove, & J. John (Eds.), *Services marketing self-portraits: Introspections, reflections, and glimpses from the experts* (pp. 173–187). Chicago: American Marketing Association.

Schneider, B., & Bowen, D. E. (1985). Employee and customer perceptions of service in banks: Replication and extension. *Journal of Applied Psychology, 70,* 423–433.

Schneider, B., & Bowen, D. E. (1993). The service organization: Human resources management is crucial. *Organizational Dynamics, 21,* 39–52.

Schneider, B., & Bowen, D. E. (1995). *Winning the service game.* Boston, MA: Harvard Business School Press.

Schneider, B., Parkington, J. J., & Buxton, V. M. (1980). Employee and customer perceptions of service in banks. *Administrative Science Quarterly, 25,* 252–267.

Schneider, B., White, S. S., & Paul, M. C. (1998). Linking service climate and customer perceptions of service quality in banks: Test of a causal model. *Journal of Applied Psychology, 83*(2), 150–163.

Shostack, G. L. (1987). Service positioning through structural change. *Journal of Marketing, 51,* 34–43.

Spechler, J. W. (1993). *Managing quality in America's most admired companies.* San Francisco: Berrett-Kohler.

Taguchi, G. (1993). *Taguchi on robust technology development: Bringing quality engineering upstream.* New York: ASME.

White, S., & Schneider, B. (2000). Climbing the advocacy ladder: The impact of disconfirmation of service expectations on customers' behavioral intentions. *Journal of Services Research, 2*(3), 240–253.

Wiley, J. W. (1991). Customer satisfaction and employee opinions: A supportive work environment and its financial cost. *Human Resources Planning, 14,* 117–127.

Winkleman, M., Schultz, D., Edelman, D., & Silverstein, M. (1993). Up close and personal. *Journal of Business Strategy, 14*(4), 23–31.

Yuskavage, R. E. (1996, August). Improved estimates of gross product by industry, 1959–94. *Survey of Current Business,* pp. 133–155.

Zeithaml, V. A., & Bitner, M. J. (2000). *Services marketing: Integrating customer focus across the firm* (2nd ed.). Boston, MA: McGraw-Hill.

Zeithaml, V., Parasuraman, A., & Berry, L. L. (1990). *Delivering service quality.* New York: Free Press.

2

Conceptualization and Measurement of Service Quality

"What's the best way to define service quality?" and "What's the best way to measure it?" were questions that faced Parasuraman, Zeithaml, and Berry (1985, 1988) as they launched their program of research dedicated to understanding service quality. Although the importance of studying services separately from goods was becoming apparent in the early 1980s, no one had seriously dedicated a program of research to answering these questions. The program launched by Parasuraman et al. resulted in the development of a model and accompanying measure of service quality called SERVQUAL (Parasuraman, Zeithaml, & Berry, 1985, 1988). Their approach to defining and measuring service quality still pervades much of the service quality literature today, and SERVQUAL remains a very popular—if not the most popular—measure of service quality for researchers and practitioners (Zeithaml & Bitner, 2000). We therefore discuss SERVQUAL in considerable detail in this chapter.

One of the primary contributions of SERVQUAL has been the issues that it has raised and forced the services management field to address. There is still debate and change surrounding many of the concepts of service quality, which serves to demonstrate the youth of the services field. It is important to keep in mind that the general body of service quality literature as a definable discipline has existed for only a few decades. Because the literature has not arrived at a state of agreement on many of the issues presented in this chapter, we feel it is important to review several different perspectives—both old and new, and from several different conceptual and empirical approaches. The current chapter presents our take on how the different viewpoints can be combined for a unified picture of defining and measuring service quality.

The issues that we have chosen to discuss below are those that we see as key for understanding the conceptual and operational struggles that have surrounded the field of service quality. This is not to say that other fields have not struggled with similar issues or that the services literature has not been informed by these other fields. For example, just as the relationships between the facets or dimensions of service quality and overall service quality have been studied, so have the relationships between the facets or dimensions of employee job satisfaction and overall job satisfaction been investigated. Still, even though it has been able to draw from work done in other areas, much of the services field's growth and development has come from grappling with issues such as those discussed below.

Dimensions of Service Quality

As with any field, one of the first challenges faced in the area of service quality was getting a handle on exactly what it meant. That is, what things do people consider in figuring out if service was good or bad? Of course, one possibility is that people think about service experiences as wholes, without considering multiple aspects of service at all. This position has not been as well supported as the alternative—that people base their evaluations of service quality on multiple aspects of their service experience. The measurement of service quality has typically proceeded under the implicit, if not explicit, assumption that it is a multidimensional construct (Gummesson, 1992; Parasuraman, Zeithaml, & Berry, 1985, 1988; White & Schneider, 2000). In this section, we turn our attention to what the facets of service quality might be. As will become clear, and as we noted in Chapter 1, the dimensions of service quality that have emerged tend to focus on the process aspect of service *delivery*, much more so than on the technical outcomes associated with the services.[1]

Given the premise that there are multiple service quality dimensions, the next question to ask is whether there is consistency in the dimensions considered across people and across different types of services. That is, is every individual unique in what he or she looks for in service delivery as a basis for a service quality judgment or is there some consistency across people in the experiences they find salient? Even if people agree on what they look for in one type of service, does this generalize to other types of service delivery experiences? Let's look at what happens when different service marketing researchers approach the issue of defining and measuring the dimensions of service quality.

SERVQUAL Dimensions

We will begin with a discussion of the dimensions in the SERVQUAL model of service quality. Again, because of its central importance and its widespread use in services research, we will spend more time examining the development of research on this set of dimensions than the others that we review. In examining the dimensionality of service quality, Parasuraman, Zeithaml, and Berry (1985, 1988) started at the beginning—by talking to customers. One important finding that emerged from this early qualitative research was support for the idea of consistency across services in the types of factors that people considered in evaluating service quality. Several common themes emerged across their customer focus groups in terms of the facets of service that customers considered in judging the quality of a service, and the authors identified ten dimensions on which customers evaluated service quality in general (Tangibles, Reliability, Responsiveness, Competence, Courtesy, Credibility, Security, Access, Communication, and Understanding the Customer). What was interesting about this list was its focus on service delivery issues.

A SERVQUAL survey measure was subsequently designed to collect quantitative data on these dimensions. Beginning with a 200-item survey, the authors engaged in an iterative process of survey administration, factor analysis, and item elimination to arrive at their factor structure for service quality.[2] Through this series of revisions and refinements, Parasuraman et al. arrived at a 22-item, five-factor version of SERVQUAL (Parasuraman, Zeithaml, & Berry, 1985, 1988, 1994a, 1994b; Zeithaml, Berry, & Parasuraman, 1993; Zeithaml, Parasuraman, & Berry, 1990). The dimensions of the survey with abstracted definitions are presented in Table 2.1.

It would be great to be able to say that this was the final word on the dimensionality of SERVQUAL. That would mean all work using the SERVQUAL measure all fit neatly into the same five-factor model. However, this is not the case. Several authors who have employed the SERVQUAL items in their studies have found as few as one or two factors (Babakus & Boller, 1992; Cronin & Taylor, 1992;

Table 2.1   SERVQUAL Dimensions and Definitions

Dimension	Definition
Reliability	Delivering the promised performance dependably and accurately
Tangibles	Appearance of the organization's facilities, employees, equipment, and communication materials
Responsiveness	Willingness of the organization to provide prompt service and help customers
Assurance (Combination of items designed originally to assess Competence, Courtesy, Credibility, and Security)	Ability of the organization's employees to inspire trust and confidence in the organization through their knowledge and courtesy
Empathy (Combination of items designed originally to assess Access, Communication, and Understanding the Customer)	Personalized attention given to a customer

White & Schneider, 2000).[3] To further complicate matters, other researchers have argued for more than five factors. For example, Carman (1990) proposed that the original ten dimensions might have been better reduced to seven or eight factors rather than five, and Gummesson (1992) makes the point that he finds Parasuraman at al.'s original ten dimensions easier to discuss with managers than the final five.

Of course, many of these differences might be due in part to changes that authors make to the survey (e.g., adding or rewording items, changing response scales) or the way they analyze the data (e.g., using different factor analysis methods). However, even the original authors of SERVQUAL have had some difficulty in replicating the five-factor structure that the survey was designed to reflect. For example, Parasuraman, Berry, and Zeithaml (1991a) found Tangibles splitting into two factors (physical facilities/equipment and employees/communication materials), while Responsiveness and Assurance loaded onto one.

The problems in replicating SERVQUAL's five-factor structure have led some researchers to suggest that there is no universal set of factors that are relevant across service industries (Babakus & Boller, 1992; Cronin & Taylor, 1992). Babakus and Boller (1992) expressed the following view:

It may not be fruitful to pursue the development of a standard measurement scale applicable to a wide variety of services. The domain of service quality may be factorially complex in some industries and very simple and unidimensional in others. As such, measures designed for specific service industries may be a more viable research strategy to pursue. (p. 265)

Several authors have followed the path of developing industry-specific instruments, leading to DINESERV for restaurants (Stevens, Knutson, & Patton, 1995), LODGSERV for lodging properties (Knutson, Stevens, Wullaert, Patton, & Yokoyama, 1990), and the Retail Service Quality Scale for retailing industries (Dabholkar, Thorpe, & Rentz, 1996).

In sum, SERVQUAL does not appear to be universally applicable to all situations without modification. While Parasuraman et al. intended the measure to be comprehensive and to apply to a wide variety of services industries, they have always recognized the potential need to modify or supplement the survey. The dimensions of Reliability, Tangibles, Responsiveness, Assurance, and Empathy may be too broad for some service industries, but too narrow for others. A process similar to the one used to develop SERVQUAL in the first place can also be used to determine the appropriateness of SERVQUAL for a particular organization or industry and how it might need to be modified. That is, researchers could start their measurement process by using customer focus groups to identify service quality themes, developing new items or finding existing ones (e.g., SERVQUAL items) to measure the themes, and then refining the survey through statistical techniques such as factor analysis.

However, rather than modifying the basic SERVQUAL model, other approaches have also been developed that might be useful. We now turn to other scholars' conceptualizations of the dimensionality of service quality.

Grönroos's Dimensions

Grönroos (1990) derived six criteria for experienced service quality, pertaining essentially only to the functional (delivery) rather than the technical (service product) issues. The six dimensions, with their definitions, are presented in Table 2.2.

In many ways, the dimensions proposed by Grönroos (1990) are similar to those represented in the SERVQUAL typology. For example, they both have dimensions of Reliability. Furthermore, the themes of

Table 2.2   Grönroos's Dimensions of Perceived Service Quality

Dimension	Definition
Professionalism and Skills	Do the employees, physical resources, and operational systems of the organization have the knowledge and skills to solve customer problems in a professional way?
Attitudes and Behaviors	Do the service employees (contact persons) show concern for customers and interest in solving their problems in a friendly and spontaneous way?
Accessibility and Flexibility	Is the service provider (e.g., its location, operating hours, employees, operational systems) designed so that customers can access the service easily and so that the provider can adjust to the demands and wishes of a customer in a flexible way?
Reliability and Trustworthiness	Do the customers know that they can rely on the service provider, its employees, and its systems to keep promises and perform with the best interest of the customer at heart?
Recovery	Do the customers realize that whenever something goes wrong or something unpredictable happens, the service provider will immediately take steps to keep the customer in control and to find an acceptable new solution?
Reputation and Credibility	Do the customers believe that the operations of the service provider can be trusted and give adequate value for the money, and that it stands for good performance and values which can be shared by customers and the service provider?[a]

SOURCE: From Grönroos, Christian. *Service Quality: Research Perspectives* (1990). Adapted with permission.

NOTE: a. Grönroos denotes this dimension as an "image-related" one. An organization's corporate or local image with customers can influence how they perceive the other aspects of quality; it is essentially a filter. For example, Grönroos raises the possibility that people will be more inclined to forgive mistakes in a company with a good reputation for quality than one with a bad reputation.

trusting in the organization and the knowledge of its people to deliver quality service that are represented in Grönroos's Reputation/ Credibility and Professionalism/Skills dimensions can be found in the SERVQUAL dimension of Assurance. In addition, the Grönroos Attitudes and Behavior dimension reflects the same idea of caring for the customer that is seen in SERVQUAL's Empathy dimension. However, while SERVQUAL covers the issue of convenient operating hours (under the Empathy dimension), it does not focus as much attention on it as Grönroos's dimension of Accessibility and Flexibility.

Service Recovery. Elements of Grönroos's fifth dimension of Recovery can be seen in the SERVQUAL dimension of Responsiveness, focusing on responding to customer problems and complaints. Just as Grönroos broke Recovery out as its own dimension, other service researchers have focused their attention on the topic of service recovery or responses to incidents where service has failed (e.g., an airline flight is cancelled, tickets are issued for the wrong date, etc.). For example, Bitner and her colleagues conducted a study of how organizations responded to service failures (Bitner, Booms, & Tetreault, 1990). These authors found that when the customers felt the organizations managed to recover well, customers remembered the failed service encounters favorably. Handling the problem "well" frequently entailed compensation for an inconvenience, such as giving people available VIP hotel suites when their reservations were lost. However, "Even acknowledging the problem, explaining why the service is unavailable and assisting the customer in solving the problem by suggesting possible options can be enough to cause the customer to remember the event favorably" (Bitner et al., 1990, p. 76).

Also supporting the value of effective service recovery, studies have found that when a complaining customer is persuaded to stay with an organization, this customer can be more loyal to the organization than before the complaint (Fornell & Wernerfelt, 1987, 1988). The work that has been conducted in the area of service recovery suggests that it is an important element of the service delivery process, and perhaps deserves to be studied as its own dimension, as Grönroos (1990) proposed.[4]

Gummesson's Dimensions

Grönroos's decision to consider Recovery as its own dimension illustrates how certain researchers tend to accord more importance to some dimensions compared with others. For example, Gummesson (1992) developed a typology of service dimensions that focuses more on the tangible aspects of service than does SERVQUAL or Grönroos' (1990) typology. Gummesson presented the idea that service offerings could be evaluated in terms of three elements: the service element, the tangibles element, and—increasingly—the software or information technology element. He presented the example that the quality of an airline flight is dependent on the interactions of airline employees with the passengers (service), the physical aircraft (tangibles), and the computers that control and assist in the delivery of service (software). He then proceeded to list dimensions that customers might use to evaluate each of the elements of the service experience. These are shown in Table 2.3. Obviously, Table 2.3 focuses much more on the technical issues involved in service than did Grönroos or Parasuraman et al.

For what he called the service element, Gummesson largely agreed with the SERVQUAL research and proposed that customers would evaluate service in terms of reliability, responsiveness, assurance, and empathy. Tangibles, however, was broken out as its own element of the service experience and given more attention than it has typically been given in the SERVQUAL research. Gummesson presented numerous dimensions on which customers might evaluate the tangible element of their service experience. The dimensions derived from three perspectives of the tangibles elements: the manufacturing/goods perspective (Garvin, 1988), a psychological perspective concerned with aspects of tangibility that affect consumers' ability to interact with products in everyday life (Norman, 1988), and an environmental perspective that addresses the impact of the larger physical environment of the service experience on the evaluation of it (Baker, 1986). Finally, Gummesson argues for a separate software element to service delivery, holding that (a) many service firms are dependent on computer systems (e.g., telecommunications, reservations systems, etc.) and (b) customers often interact with computers and software in obtaining service (e.g., automated telephone systems, automatic teller machines, etc.).

Tangibles. By breaking down the tangibles component of service quality into such detail, Gummesson indicates his belief that it is an important aspect of the service delivery process. While Parasuraman, Berry, and Zeithaml (1991a) have found that people tend to consider Tangibles the least important of the SERVQUAL dimensions, there is some evidence that it is more important than it is sometimes given credit for. For example, White and Schneider (2000) found that the tangible elements of service did play a substantial role in affecting customer attitudes and behaviors. Bitner (1992) has also focused on the importance of tangibles in her work on servicescapes—the physical facilities where service is delivered. The surroundings in which services are delivered can impact the way people perceive the organization and the service it delivers as well as their feelings toward the organization (Zeithaml & Bitner, 2000). Thus, while Tangibles may often be rated as less important than other dimensions in the SERVQUAL typology, it is by no means an

Table 2.3   Gummesson's Typology of Service Dimensions

Dimensions of Customer-Perceived Quality of Total Offering		
For Service Elements Reliability Responsiveness Assurance Empathy		
For Tangible Elements		
Goods Perspective	*Psychological Perspective*	*Environmental Perspective*
Reliability (probability of malfunctioning)	Visibility (seeing all important aspects of a product properly)	Ambient factors (background features customers may or may not be aware of)
Performance (primary characteristics of core product)	Mapping (relation between a control and the reaction to the control)	Functionality (factors contributing to use of product)
Features (extras)	Affordance (the purposes the product allows)	Aesthetics (factors contributing to appearance of product)
Conformance (match between specifications and performance)	Constraints (factors limiting what can be done with a product)	Service personnel (e.g., the number, appearance, behavior of people)
Serviceability (easy of repair and maintenance)	Customer control (control over product's functioning)	Other customers
Aesthetics (refers to exterior design, task, smell, touch, etc.)	Knowledge needed (information necessary to use product)	Other people
	Feedback (confirmation of results of actions)	
For Software Elements Reliability (ability to function correctly under different circumstances) Extendability (ability of software to adapt to new specifications) Integrity (ability to protect against unauthorized access) User friendliness (ease of learning to operate software)		

SOURCE: Originally published by JAI Press, 1992. Copyright © 2003 by T.A. Swartz, D. E. Bowen, and S.W. Brown. Used by permission.

insignificant component of service and can affect the ways customers react to the service delivery process.

Rust, Zahorik, and Keiningham (1996)

The typologies of service quality that we have presented to this point (Parasuraman et al.'s SERVQUAL; Grönroos, 1990; Gummesson, 1992) have all been organized according to the customers' point of view. That is, they define and measure service quality from the customers' perspective. Rust, Zahorik, and Keiningham (1996) also adhere to the idea of defining service quality by asking customers about the service they receive, but they argue that the dimensions of service quality to be measured should relate to the business processes of the organization—sales, billing, product, and the rest. The logic of organizing customer surveys around business processes is to facilitate changes on the basis of the customer survey data generated. Responsibility and ownership for business processes are much more easily assessed than is responsibility for a dimension such as Empathy. By measuring customer perceptions in terms of business processes, there is little ambiguity about who should take charge of changes suggested by customer surveys—and there is therefore a greater likelihood of change. It should be noted that the authors still recommend customer focus groups in order to ensure that no major areas of concern are omitted from customer surveys, as well as to make sure that survey items are worded in the customers' terminology.

Tailoring Service Quality Surveys to Specific Situations

The typologies of service dimensions that have been presented are intended to serve only as frameworks for people measuring service quality. That is, they were designed to be modified and changed to fit the needs of specific contexts. These changes might entail including new dimensions to cover aspects of service unique to a particular firm or industry, or—in the case of SERVQUAL—it might mean editing the wording of items.

From the very first, Parasuraman, Zeithaml, and Berry (1988) recognized that SERVQUAL would not be adequate to measure services in all organizations and all industries without some modification. They made the point that "it provides a basic skeleton . . . encompassing statements for each of the five service-quality dimensions. The skeleton, when necessary, can be adapted or supplemented to fit the characteristics or specific research needs of a particular organization" (Parasuraman, Zeithaml, & Berry, 1988, pp. 30–31). For example, Schneider and Bowen (1985) included a service quality dimension labeled Employee Morale in their customer service survey for bank customers to capture customer perceptions of employee's attitudes. While SERVQUAL addresses how employees interact with customers, it does not address the metalevel issue of how customers "read" employee attitudes, something Schneider (1980) found customers of bank branches talk about when they are asked to discuss service quality. Similarly, Dabholkar et al. (1996) proposed a dimension of Policy to measure how customer perceptions of store policy (e.g., credit and charge account policies) affected service quality in a retail environment.

Content vs. Form. For many researchers, the service dimensions covered by SERVQUAL are adequate for measuring service quality. However, the precise way in which the dimensions are measured—the content and wording of the items—may be insufficient. This raises the distinction between the general content and specific form of service quality measures (Gummesson, 1992; Schneider & Bowen, 1995).

Knowing the SERVQUAL dimensions provides an indication of what the content of a service quality measure might be (i.e., the kinds of service quality issues that organizations should address). However, it remains for each organization to determine what each of the dimensions means for its own particular service delivery process, and what form the dimensions should take (Schneider & Bowen, 1995). In other words, Tangibles might refer to the appearance of written materials for a travel agent, but to the state of an automatic teller machine for a bank. The content remains the same in its focus on visible aspects of the service delivery process, but the form of the dimension is very different for the two industries. Each dimension and item in SERVQUAL can be made specific for a particular industry or organization. For example, DINESERV is an instrument built on the basis of SERVQUAL to measure service quality in the restaurant industry (Stevens et al., 1995). DINESERV translated the SERVQUAL item of "Employees of XYZ have the knowledge to answer your questions" (tapping the Assurance dimension) to "[XYZ] has personnel who are both able and willing to give you information about menu items, their ingredients, and methods of preparation."

Summary

Our sense is that, for many purposes, the SERVQUAL measure and its underlying dimensions can usefully serve as a base for the development of service quality surveys in many settings and in many industries. But notice the focus on the words "base for": We are of the opinion that it is more important to capture the service quality issues for a particular organization or industry than it is to slavishly rely on the published version of SERVQUAL—and this is in agreement with the way Parasuraman, Zeithaml, and Berry (1988) proposed the measure be used. Of particular importance in this regard is the relative sparseness of items having to do with Tangibles in SERVQUAL; one needs to ensure that the tangibles issues for a service quality measurement are adequately covered, as Gummesson (1992) makes clear. A useful rule of thumb might be that, as the tangible component(s) of a service increase in salience, the number and variety of items used to assess tangibles should also be increased. Of course, this principle also applies to the other dimensions.

This is not an issue unique to the measurement of service quality. All measures of phenomena that we think and believe exist are made by us—they are not handed down from Mt. Sinai with a known number of dimensions, forever unchangeable. If we believe something exists, then it exists in some amount and it can be measured, but the number of dimensions required to capture the phenomenon can be infinite, depending on the purpose of the measurement, the level of abstraction at which the phenomenon is conceptualized, and so forth. In some instances, a global measure of overall service quality suffices; in other circumstances, it may be necessary to assess 10 or 12 dimensions to capture what is going on. We have provided here some thoughts on this dimensionality and we urge researchers to ensure that the measures they use adequately cover the relevant dimensions in any specific project.

Gap Models and the Role
of Expectations in Service Quality

In our discussion of service quality dimensionality above, we have glossed over a central issue in the service quality literature: the gap model versus the perceptions model. In their initial qualitative work (e.g., Parasuraman, Zeithaml, & Berry, 1988), found that the focus groups they interviewed were in agreement in evaluating service quality relative to their expectations for the service. Specifically, they found that people based their service quality judgments on the "gap" that existed between their perceptions of what happened during the service transaction and their expectations for how the service transaction should have occurred. This led SERVQUAL to adopt a so-called gap-model approach to service quality, measuring it as the difference (i.e., gap) between service quality perceptions and service quality expectations. Another way of discussing this gap is as the extent to which expectations were disconfirmed. Expectations can be disconfirmed positively (better than expected service) or negatively (worse than expected service).

Certainly, the SERVQUAL authors are not alone in including expectations in their treatment of service quality. Consider the following definitions:

1. "Quality is a consumer-generated comparative judgment, since individuals have no implicit sense of quality unless a standard of comparison is provided" (Oliver, 1997, p. 163).

2. Quality is "the extent in which the service, the service process and the service organization can satisfy the expectations of the user" (Kasper, van Helsdingen, & de Vries, 1999, p. 188).

3. "Perceived service quality is the result of the consumer's comparison of expected service with perceived service" (Bojanic, 1991, p. 29).

4. Service quality is "the outcome of a process in which consumers' expectations for the service are compared with their perceptions of the service actually delivered" (Mangold & Babakus, 1991, p. 60).

A clear theme running through these definitions is the role of expectations in determining judgments about quality. (While we typically refer to expectations in general terms, a great deal of research has been conducted to further explicate this construct. Additional information on expectations can be found in Box 2.1.)

Box 2.1   Conceptualizing and Measuring Expectations

What Are Different Types of Expectations?

- Predictive: How an organization *will* perform or what customers believe (predict) will actually happen in their encounter.

(Continued)

Box 2.1   Continued

- Normative: What people believe *should* happen in an organization, whether or not they believe that it actually will (*I should be seated at the time of my dinner reservation, whether or not I believe I actually will be*).

- Excellence: How an *excellent* service organization should perform. The excellent organization does not have to be the one in question or even another real organization; respondents can use their imaginations to create an organization on which to base their expectations of excellence (Parasuraman, Berry, & Zeithaml, 1993).

- Adequate: Expectations for the minimum level of performance they would be willing to accept.

Parasuraman, Zeithaml, and Berry (Parasuraman, Zeithaml, & Berry, 1994a; Zeithaml, Parasuraman, & Berry, 1993) have suggested that the difference between someone's view of how an excellent organization should perform and the minimum he or she is willing to accept is a "zone of tolerance" for service quality (Coyne, 1989; Oliva, Oliver, & MacMillan, 1992; Parasuraman, Berry, & Zeithaml, 1991b; Storbacka, Strandvik, & Grönroos, 1994). This reflects the idea that customers are likely willing to absorb some deviations from their expectations in both positive and negative directions before deciding that the service is no longer adequate, but rather is either desired or unacceptable (Parasuraman, Berry, & Zeithaml, 1991a).

What Does It Mean to Exceed Expectations?

- Vector attributes: A vector attribute represents a positive linear relationship between the level of the attribute and service quality. There is no such thing as too much; more is always better. (Brown, Churchill, & Peter, 1993, refer to these as "motherhood" variables.) The prevailing assumption in the service quality literature is that service attributes are vector attributes, where higher and higher performance on the attribute is better.

- Ideal point attributes: An ideal point is the performance level beyond which a service attribute loses its utility. For ideal point attributes, performance beyond a certain level (the ideal point) reduces quality. In other words, people might want more Empathy—but only to a point. Beyond that point, personal attention might be seen as intrusive and annoying. Thus increasing Empathy beyond its ideal point level would actually reduce service quality.

Box 2.1   Continued

Distinguishing ideal point attributes from vector attributes has surfaced in the service quality literature because of its implications for the measurement of service quality. In particular, it casts doubt on the common interpretation of exceeding expectations (i.e., positive P-E scores) as beneficial to service quality. However, it may be that not all service quality attributes are vector attributes, and that sometimes exceeding expectations can actually hurt service quality.

Teas examined this issue in his 1993 study. Teas found that about 40% of respondents did not expect the maximum level of service from an organization, and that 7% would experience disutility beyond a given level of service. These findings suggest that there are occasions when exceeding expectations can be detrimental to service quality rather than beneficial, as is usually thought. While his empirical results indicate that this may not be the case very often, they suggest that it does occur. For example, Sutton and Rafaeli's (1988) finding that the norm in busy convenience stores was for employees to display fewer pleasant emotions toward customers might be reflective of an ideal point attribute in action. In busy convenience store settings, customers wanted fewer smiles and more efficiency; this would argue against greater displays of "pleasant emotions"—or what might be termed Empathy in SERVQUAL terms. While some level of personalized attention was desirable, more was not better.

The current question for service researchers is to determine how big of an issue ideal point attributes might be. Parasuraman, Zeithaml, and Berry (1994b) maintain that most service quality attributes probably follow the vector-attribute model, and have held that determining the magnitude of the problem is an empirical question. However, no conclusive studies have been conducted as yet. Thus it is important to keep in mind in evaluating service quality that some attributes might function as ideal point attributes.

The SERVQUAL survey provides one method of measuring service quality as a relation between perceptions and expectations. In early versions of SERVQUAL, respondents first indicated their *expectations* for service in terms of what firms in a service industry *should* be doing (e.g., with respect to delivering service on time). Second, they indicated their *perceptions* of what actually happened by answering all survey items a second time in terms of what the particular firm being evaluated *was* doing. Following the logic of the gap model of service quality, the authors then computed difference scores for each survey item by subtracting customers' expectations from their perceptions (P-E scores). These gap (difference) scores served as the basis for the factor analyses described earlier.

Gap Scores and Perceptions-Only in Assessing Service Quality

Of course, although their theoretical work supported the use of gap scores, several researchers have also argued against the use of gap scores in measuring service quality. In particular, Cronin and Taylor (1992) have argued against the P-E formulation of SERVQUAL in favor of measuring only perceptions of the service delivery experience. Using the SERVQUAL items, they labeled their perceptions-only measure SERVPERF. They found that perceptions of service performance better predicted an overall service quality judgment than did gap scores that combined perceptions and expectations.

Furthermore, several researchers have argued that perception-only measures do not have the same statistical problems as gap scores. As a general rule, gap scores tend to suffer from poor statistical properties, including poor reliability, questionable validity (particularly in terms of showing a construct is distinct from other constructs, which is known as discriminant validity), and restricted variance (making it hard to demonstrate relationships with other variables; Babakus & Boller, 1992; Brown, Churchill, & Peter, 1993; Cronin & Taylor, 1992).[5] In their examination of difference scores, Brown et al. (1993) argued that all of these problems with gap scores definitely manifest themselves in SERVQUAL.

Parasuraman, Zeithaml, and Berry (1994a) have attempted to address the statistical issues surrounding the use of difference scores in SERVQUAL. Specifically, they conducted a study in which they compared the use of difference scores to a direct measure of how perceptions compared to expectations. This direct measure asked respondents to indicate on a single nine-point scale how they believed the quality of service they were offered compared to the level of service that they desired (i.e., was service lower than, same as, or higher than desired service level). They found that the difference scores performed as well on all psychometric criteria as the direct measures, with the exception of being able to explain the variance in ratings of perceptions of overall service quality. Perceptions-only measures were superior here, as suggested by previous studies (Brown et al., 1993; Cronin & Taylor, 1992).

However, unlike the authors of the previous studies, Parasuraman, Zeithaml, and Berry (1994a) did not conclude that the perceptions-only measure was the measure of choice. They maintained that the conceptualization of service quality as a P-E gap is grounded in past theory and supported by their focus group research. They argued that the measure to be used should depend on the purpose of research being conducted:

> If maximizing predictive power is the principal objective, the perceptions-only scale is the best as it outperforms all other measures on this criterion. However, if identifying critical service shortfalls is the principal objective, the [P-E] format seems most useful; and this format also provides separate perceptions ratings for those concerned with maximizing predictive power. (Parasuraman, Zeithaml, & Berry, 1994a, p. 216)

That is, by including the measurement of expectations, managers of the service delivery process will have a better idea of which aspects of service they are expected to perform exceptionally highly on versus those where lower levels of expectations exist. Assuming that these managers will want to devote more time and energy to areas where expectations are higher, the measurement of expectations becomes diagnostically important. We agree with the conclusion that there is value in measuring both perceptions and expectations, because it allows answers to both (a) the practical question (Where are the shortfalls?) and (b) the research question (Is the P-E formulation superior to the perceptions-only formulation?).

Overall Service Quality

Defining Overall Service Quality

To this point in the chapter, we have addressed the central issues of what dimensions people may consider in evaluating service quality, as well as whether these dimensions are best measured in terms of perceptions or as P-E gap scores. However, definitions of service quality typically do not refer to assessments on specified service quality dimensions, but rather are framed in terms of global, overall evaluations. For example, a frequently cited definition of service quality is that it is *a customer's judgment of the overall excellence or superiority of a service* (Zeithaml, 1988).[6] A similar definition holds that the "sum total" of the customer's perception of the service is at the center of service quality research (Gummesson, 1992).

What are these overall judgments of service quality based on? This returns us to two of our earlier discussions: service quality dimensions and P-E gap scores. First, people's overall evaluations of service quality are typically thought to be based on their assessments of service quality dimensions (see Box 2.2 for more detail). Second, a popular school of thought holds that the degree to which expectations for service are met (or not) determines overall service quality evaluations. In other words, if a researcher measured perceptions and expectations regarding a firm's service, the difference between the two would be considered the basis for an overall service quality assessment or judgment. Thus these P-E gaps are not seen as directly defining overall service quality, but rather are seen as preceding (or mediating) such evaluations (Cronin & Taylor, 1992).

Box 2.2   Relating Overall Service Quality and Service Quality
          Dimensions

Graphically, several authors have used diagrams, such as Figure 2.1, to indicate service quality dimensions as determinants of an overall judgment. Note that the direction of the arrows in Figure 2.1 lead from the dimensions to the Perceived Service Quality factor. That is, Perceived Service Quality is the result of the dimensions.

While the idea that dimensions are determinants of overall service quality is dominant in the current services literature, another perspective could be considered. This perspective would represent overall service quality as a higher-order factor, capturing a common theme of overall quality in the dimensions. That is, a construct of overall quality could be considered to be exerting

Box 2.2   Continued

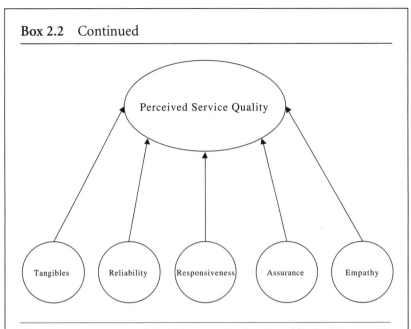

Figure 2.1   Portion of Model Presented in Cronin and Taylor (1992, p. 58)

influence on each of the service dimensions. A graphical representation of such a perspective would look something like Figure 2.2. This model was created to represent service in the retail industry (Dabholkar et al., 1996).

The model presented in Figure 2.2 differs from the model in Figure 2.1 in that the arrows connecting the dimensions and the overall service quality factor are pointing in the opposite direction. Rather than having the dimensions determining the overall service factor, the overall factor is exerting an influence on the individual dimensions (see Dabholkar et al., 1996).

Think about it this way: You go into a service setting and you emerge feeling that the quality of the service you received was pretty darn high. Then someone with a clipboard comes along and asks you to rate the service quality you just experienced, from *poor* to *excellent*. You answer "very good," and are then immediately asked to rate the specific dimensions of the service you just experienced. Lo and behold, you rate each of the dimensions of

(Continued)

Box 2.2   Continued

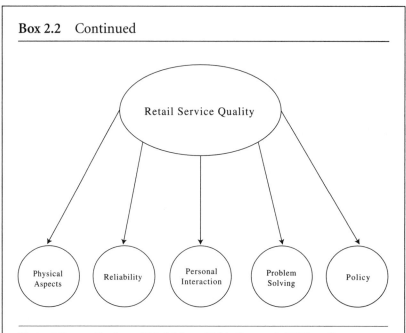

Figure 2.2   Portion of Model from Dabholkar et al. (1996, p. 6)

service quality as being "very good." A conclusion here might be that your overall impression affected the way you rated the service dimensions—with the overall judgment determining the specific judgments.

The fact is that we do not yet have enough information to say what is determining what in the relationship between overall service quality judgments and the specific dimensions of service quality. We suspect that, at the very least, the dimensions are subconsciously influencing the overall judgment because *some experience* must occur for the overall judgment to be made and research has generally proceeded under this hypothesis. From a practical standpoint, of course, the dimensions have diagnostic value. If a researcher's sole goal is to predict other constructs with a service quality measure, he or she may have no need for a more detailed measurement of service quality than an overall measure. However, if there is any interest in how to change or manipulate service quality, then it becomes important to identify the issues that could be potentially manipulated to affect the overall

---

Box 2.2   Continued

---

judgment—these are the dimensions of service quality. "An assessment of the overall performance of an organization is not enough. This provides little or no insight into the shortcomings or excellent parts of the service delivery" (Kasper et al., 1999, p. 211).

The definition of service quality as an assessment of *overall* superiority of a service is important because so little effort has gone into research on this overall or "composite" (Gummesson, 1992) judgment relative to the work that has been done on defining its factors. Practitioners (and researchers, too) typically average together responses on their surveys to define overall service quality, and most likely do not think twice about it. Below, we will present some arguments against using this averaging approach in favor of directly measuring overall service quality perceptions.

Measuring Overall Service Quality

First, while different people may rate individual dimensions of services in the same way, they may also interpret these ratings very differently. That is, two people may rate an organization as having exceeded expectations with regards to Empathy, but one may view this much more favorably than the other. This indicates a need to measure people's overall *interpretations* of scores as well as the scores themselves (Oliver, 1997), and argues against averaging together ratings on individual service quality dimensions to reflect an overall evaluation.

Also, averaging together scores on given service quality dimensions to derive an overall service quality score implies that all of the determinants of the overall judgment are known. That is, if an overall judgment is defined as the average of scores on attributes 1, 2, 3, 4, and 5, the overall judgment score will be inaccurate to the extent that dimensions 6, 7, and 8 are missing from the average. Furthermore, the relative importance of the dimensions that have been identified in determining overall service quality may not be known.

To account for the idea that different dimensions might be more or less important to different people, Zeithaml, Parasuraman, and Berry

(1990) recommend assigning importance weights to each of the service quality dimensions in analyses. The measure of importance that these authors have used entails asking respondents to divide 100 points among their five dimensions—assigning more points to the dimensions they consider to be more important. Alternatively, an overall rating of service quality could be statistically regressed onto individual dimensions, with the resulting regression coefficients serving as the weights (Kasper et al., 1999).[7] A third choice would be to obtain direct judgments of importance. For example, Cronin and Taylor (1992) and Teas (1993) asked respondents to rate the importance of the different SERVQUAL items. However, neither of these studies found any benefit to weighting item scores by importance ratings in improving the ability of the scale to predict a rating of overall service quality.

Thus including item importance ratings may increase the procedural burdens of administering service quality surveys without generating much of a return. Nonetheless, it is possible that measuring importance at an attribute or dimension level can still be worthwhile and should be undertaken (Carman, 1990; Kasper et al., 1999; Zeithaml, Parasuraman, & Berry, 1990). Certainly, it is beneficial for managers of service delivery processes to know which elements of service quality customers say are more important to them than others, which could be obtained from dividing points across the service quality dimensions. It could also be useful for managers to see what the data say are the relative weights of the several service attributes in predicting or correlating with overall service quality. Such information could be obtained from the regression approach described above.

An alternative to averaging together dimension scores to form an overall service quality score is very simple: It is common for researchers to include a single item asking participants what they think of the overall service quality at Organization XYZ. For example, in addition to administering the SERVQUAL items, Cronin and Taylor (1992) asked respondents to fill in the blank of "The quality of XYZ's services is . . ." with a response ranging from *very poor* to *excellent.* Bolton and Drew (1991) asked people, "How would you rate the overall quality of services provided by the local telephone company?" with a response scale of *poor/fair/good/excellent.*

While single-item measures have the advantage of capturing an overall judgment, they are limited in that internal consistency reliability cannot be calculated for them. Oliver (1997) therefore recommended that more effort be devoted to developing multiple-item global service quality scales. For example, Teas (1993) asked participants to rate the overall quality of the service they received on a scale of 1 (*extremely low quality*) to 10 (*extremely high quality*), as well as to rate their agreement with the statement, "XYZ provides high-quality service" (1 = *strongly disagree*; 5 = *strongly agree*). It is important in these measures to guard against including items related more to constructs of customer satisfaction or value than service quality.

Service Quality and Customer Satisfaction

The focus of this chapter to this point has been on defining and measuring service quality as defined from the consumer's point of view. An important part of the evolution of the service quality concept has been distinguishing it from the related concept of customer satisfaction. There does appear to be consensus that the two are conceptually distinct yet empirically overlapping constructs, but there is still debate about the details. (An obvious demonstration of the separability of the constructs is that service quality is only one component of a customer's level of satisfaction; for example, price likely has a direct effect on satisfaction, but it is less likely to directly affect a customer's report of overall service quality.)

In discussing overall judgments of service quality, we presented a definition of service quality as a judgment about a service's overall excellence or superiority. Customer satisfaction, on the other hand, has been defined as "a judgment that a product or service feature, or the product or service itself, provided (or is providing) a pleasurable level of consumption-related fulfillment, including levels of under- or overfulfillment" (Oliver, 1997, p. 13). That is, service quality is a consumer's judgment about the service itself, while satisfaction is more a judgment of how the service emotionally affects the consumer. Oliver (1997) explicates this distinction nicely by introducing the idea that a product must be experienced to make a satisfaction judgment, but that is not the case for determining quality judgments. For example, people might be able to state whether they think a particular restaurant is of high or low quality based solely on perceptions that they have of it formed from advertising or word of mouth, but they will not be able to state if they are satisfied with it without actually experiencing dining at the restaurant.

While service quality and customer satisfaction can be distinguished based on their conceptual definitions, an additional issue of debate has concerned the differences between the two on the issue of temporal focus. In some of the early writings that distinguished service quality from customer satisfaction (Bolton & Drew, 1991; Parasuraman, Zeithaml, & Berry, 1988), service quality judgments were viewed as global evaluations that were composites of customers' experiences with an organization (*global-level evaluations*), while satisfaction referred to evaluations of specific experiences with an organization (*encounter-specific evaluations*). In other words, a customer might refer to a particular night out at a restaurant in terms of his or her satisfaction with the experience, but refer to the restaurant itself in terms of the quality of the establishment—based on the composite of that person's experiences with that restaurant as well as others.

As with the issue of the causal direction of overall quality judgments and judgments about specific dimensions of quality, a causal conundrum exists with regard to whether satisfaction causes quality judgments or quality judgments cause satisfaction.[8] Fortunately, there appears to be good agreement on this issue: Quality judgments cause satisfaction (Loveman, 1998; Parasuraman, Zeithaml, & Berry, 1994b; Storbacka, Strandvik, & Grönroos, 1994). Based on empirical findings and the conceptual development of the service quality concept, service quality is now often believed to be the antecedent of satisfaction (Heskett, Sasser, & Schlesinger, 1997; Reidenbach & Sandifer-Smallwood, 1990; Woodside, Frey, & Daly, 1989). Or, as Kasper et al. (1999) put it: "In the literature, a debate is going on as to whether quality is an antecedent of satisfaction, or whether satisfaction is an antecedent of quality. Our position in that debate is . . . [that] quality leads to satisfaction" (p. 289).

Agreement on conceptual distinctions and causal arrows do not, unfortunately, necessarily yield agreement in terms of measurement. One sticking point in the measurement of satisfaction and quality concerns the role of expectations. (See Box 2.1 for more information on expectations.) The gap model of service quality presented earlier held that service quality judgments were the result of comparisons between perceptions of service performance and expectations for performance. What was not emphasized, however, was that this vantage point on quality as resulting from disconfirmed expectations originated in the *customer satisfaction* literature. Arguing that both service quality evaluations and customer satisfaction result from disconfirmed expectations has resulted in great confusion in distinguishing the two constructs.

One approach to clarifying the differences between service quality and customer satisfaction might involve the type of expectation involved in the disconfirmation of expectations. Typically, *predictive* expectations have been used as comparison standards in the customer satisfaction/dissatisfaction literature (Churchill & Suprenant, 1982; Oliver, 1997; Parasuraman, Zeithaml, & Berry, 1994b). That is, customer satisfaction is believed to result from a comparison of what did happen in a service experience with what customers believed (predicted) was going to happen. Service quality judgments, though, are thought to result from disconfirmations of *expectations of excellence* (e.g., Parasuraman, Zeithaml, & Berry, 1994b). It should be noted that while the predictive/excellence distinction is supported by some researchers (e.g., Oliver, 1997), it is not universally used (e.g., Bolton & Drew, 1991) and is an issue that clearly requires additional research.

Perceived service quality and customer satisfaction are obviously closely related constructs. They are both concerned with how consumers experience an organization, and we continue to believe it is useful to keep the two conceptually distinct, even though the two terms are often used interchangeably in practice. The point we would make is that the two still seem to be conceptually separate, with satisfaction being more evaluative and emotionally laden, and quality being more descriptive and factually based. We think this distinction is important and might yield some direction for their future measurement.

Approached from our proposed vantage point, the measurement of quality would be about a perception (*this is what I observe*), perhaps relative to expectations; the measurement of satisfaction would be about an evaluation (*this is what I feel*). For example, an item in SERVQUAL states that "Organization XYZ can be counted on to keep the promises it makes." This is a service quality item for us, because it is a statement of "fact" and people can report on the degree to which this happens. A satisfaction item might read "I am satisfied with the way organization XYZ keeps the promises it makes." These two items are useful for different purposes—the former for diagnosing the way the organization performs and the latter for diagnosing the way customers feel. So, depending on the purpose for which assessment of customer experiences is conducted, one will use either of the conceptual and operational perspectives—understanding, of course, that the results will be correlated but differentially useful for taking action.

Survey Development: An Integrated Perspective

What has emerged clearly from our discussions of defining and measuring service quality is that there is still considerable conceptual and empirical debate surrounding these issues. The degree of controversy in the literature makes it difficult for service quality researchers to determine how they should go about defining and operationalizing service quality in their empirical studies. After all of the discussion, it seemed appropriate for us to present the way in which we might go about developing such a measure. In this section, we will describe how we would approach this challenge. In particular, we would recommend an approach similar to that adopted by Dabholkar et al. (1996) in their efforts to design a service quality measure for the retail service industry. We will refer to their work throughout this section of the chapter.

Conducting Focus Groups

Earlier, we reviewed the topic of service quality's dimensionality and mentioned that the SERVQUAL dimensions may or may not be sufficient for a particular industry or organization. The question that presents itself is how to determine if the five SERVQUAL dimensions need to be modified or supplemented. At this point, the use of focus groups comes into play. Talking to individual customers through focus groups is recommended as a way to generate the qualitative data that is a good starting point for developing quantitative measures of service quality (Dabholkar et al., 19961; Kasper et al., 1999; Zeithaml & Bitner, 2000). Thus, just as the original SERVQUAL authors used focus groups to determine the themes that they wanted their service quality survey to cover, focus groups remain a good way to elicit issues that are of concern to customers.

Question-and-answer sessions, informal discussions, or such procedures as the critical incident technique (CIT; see Bitner et al., 1990), in which customers are asked to provide examples of positive and negative experiences, are potential ways to obtain information from customers. In the focus groups that Parasuraman et al. conducted for SERVQUAL, they asked some questions directly of customers (what service quality meant to them, what factors they considered in evaluating service quality, what their expectations were for service performance), and they also employed the CIT to elicit examples of when customers were satisfied with service and when they were not. Given the past work that has been done on service quality and identifying its dimensions, focus group participants could be asked for their opinions on the adequacy of various typologies of service that have been developed. This could provide a starting point and direction for focus group discussions.

Of course, other techniques besides focus groups can be used to gain a sense of service issues from the customer's perspective. For example, customers do not have to be gathered together in a focus group, but could be approached one-on-one and asked to take five minutes to talk about service issues (Schneider, 1973). In-depth interviews conducted with individual customers are also an option for uncovering service issues that customers are concerned about. Another possible technique for learning about customer views on service was adopted by Dabholkar et al. (1996), in what they termed a "tracking" method. They asked individual customers to use a portable microphone and tape recorder to record their thoughts about their service experience as they were experiencing it. This is a technique frequently used in market research with products, especially when people are shopping in supermarkets, and we think it is one that could be adapted to good advantage for services research.

Finding Themes in Focus Group Data

Once the initial data have been collected, the comments generated by customers can be subjected to content analysis to determine if there are underlying themes to them. Content analysis is a process for detecting themes that underlie separate bits of information. For example, Parasuraman, Zeithaml, and Berry, (1988) had hundreds of expressions of the bases customers used for judging service quality and classified them through content analysis into the 10 original dimensions they used as a basis for the first set of items in SERVQUAL. Since developing the coding scheme used for the content analysis can be one of the most challenging aspects of the process, past literature can serve as a useful guide here. In particular, the SERVQUAL themes (the original ten or the final five) might serve as an initial coding scheme for the customer responses. Multiple coders would then independently code the data into the categories to check the reliability of the coding.

If these themes prove to be inadequate (e.g., many comments remain uncoded under the SERVQUAL scheme and/or the multiple coders cannot agree), additional coding categories can be added—potentially drawing from other authors' typologies of service reviewed earlier for the additional categories (Grönroos, 1990; Gummesson, 1992). Of course, it is also possible to take a less formal approach to the focus group data, and simply "eyeball" the data to determine the categories of service that are represented. This is certainly faster and easier, but of course the results are much less reliable than a formal coding process by multiple independent coders.

Developing Service Quality Surveys

Next, survey items should be developed to reflect the themes uncovered in the focus group discussion. By developing a survey, quantitative measures can be created from the qualitative focus group data. Quantitative measures, in turn, are important in the research process, because they allow statistical analyses and hypothesis testing of a much more refined nature than the qualitative data. Again, as with the focus groups, the past literature on service quality can serve as a guide in the process of developing survey items. If the SERVQUAL dimensions provided adequate coverage of the service themes revealed in the focus groups, then the SERVQUAL items could be used and no further work would need to be done. Dabholkar et al. (1996) used many of the SERVQUAL items in their research, although they supplemented the items with 11 of their own. Of course, whatever items are used should be modified to reflect the specific organization or industry being studied. For example, if the organization being studied is a mail-order company or a call center, the SERVQUAL items should be modified to omit questions about the appearance of employees. In addition, the items can be tailored to specific organizations by using terminology specific to the organization (e.g., use the word "catalog" rather than "brochures" when discussing a mail-order company). If, however, additional dimensions were needed in coding the focus group data, new items must be developed. Past service quality surveys that have been developed can certainly serve as a guide in this process (Dabholkar et al., 1996; Knutson et al., 1990; Stevens et al., 1995).

Based on our earlier review, we would also include some sort of global service quality measure in the survey. As mentioned previously, many researchers use single items, such as "How would you rate the quality of service at XYZ?" but multiple item scales are preferable.

The next step in developing the service quality measure is to determine whether both expectations and perceptions of service performance should be measured, or only performance. As we stated earlier, we would include both. Although perceptions-only measures have been shown to demonstrate better predictive validity than P-E measures (Cronin & Taylor, 1992; Parasuraman, Zeithaml, & Berry, 1994a), the P-E measures do seem to yield richer and more informative data, and perceptions can still be studied alone, if that is desired. Furthermore, in including an expectations measure, we would recommend following the Parasuraman et al. suggestion of measuring both an adequate and desired level of service. Again, the more information a researcher can obtain from customers, the greater his or her understanding of the customers' attitudes on the subject at hand. We would also agree with Parasuraman et al. that expectations should be measured as what excellent organizations *should* do. Efforts to address Teas's (1993) caution about the potential for some service attributes to be ideal point attributes might also be taken into account by asking participants to identify the ideal points as well as expectations.

Once the items have been developed and translated into expectations (and ideal points) and perceptions forms, the layout of the survey can be determined. The original version of SERVQUAL asked each participant to answer the 22 expectation items, and then to answer 22 perception items. This is really the only feasible way of gaining separate information about expectations and perceptions. While it might be possible to obtain direct measures of perceptions relative to expectations, these lose the diagnostic value of separate measures (Parasuraman, Zeithaml, & Berry, 1994a). One recommendation that Parasuraman et al. made to ease the burden on respondents of answering all questions twice (or three times, if ideal points are included) is to list each item once, and place the expectations and perceptions rating scales side by side. We note parenthetically that asking about the same issue with two or more frames of reference (for example, asking about expectations, perceptions, and ideals for each of the SERVQUAL items) has some advantages, but there are two distinct disadvantages. First, respondents must reply to the questions many times. Second, there are known correlations among the survey items introduced by having respondents respond to the same items. That is, a result of the sequential responding to the same items is that the responses are highly correlated—a feature that is not usually useful for the later stage of data analysis. Some (e.g., Carman, 1990) advise against the frequent collection of expectations data, with preferences for the performance data in using SERVQUAL.[9]

After the survey items have been developed, they should be reviewed with a sample of customers. First, these customers should be able to give their opinions on whether the items adequately cover the service issues that are relevant to them. Thus having a sample of people review the items can speak to the content validity of the survey (e.g., Babakus & Boller, 1992). In addition, reviewing the items with a sample of customers should allow any wording problems with the items or directions to be clarified.

Factor Analyzing Service Quality Survey Data

Once the survey has been developed, it can be administered to a sample of customers of an organization. The data collected can then be used to determine if the items are measuring the service themes that they were designed to measure. A confirmatory factor analysis can be conducted to shed light on this.[10] Of course, there have been issues raised with factor analyzing P-E gap scores (e.g., Carman, 1990; Cronin & Taylor, 1992), and researchers may want to guard against this. One solution to this problem might be to begin by factor analyzing only the perception scores of respondents (Dabholkar et al., 1996). Then, if the confirmatory factor analysis of the perception scores adequately fit the theoretical factor structure of the survey, a second confirmatory factor analysis could be conducted using the P-E gap scores. The factor structures yielded by each of these analyses could then be compared to determine how similar they were.

If the confirmatory factor analyses indicate an acceptable fit to the theoretical factor structure of the survey, an exploratory factor analysis would not be necessary. If, however, the confirmatory factor analyses suggest that the theoretical factor structure was not supported by the data, an exploratory factor analysis can help determine what the factor structure of the data actually is. In conducting an exploratory factor analysis with the items in question, it is important to remember that the dimensions of service quality are likely to be correlated with one another.[11] Thus an oblique rotation of factors, allowing for correlated dimensions, is appropriate for factor analyzing service quality items (Cronin & Taylor, 1992, 1994; Parasuraman, Zeithaml, & Berry, 1988, 1994b). The factor analysis procedure could suggest that certain items be dropped from the survey, because they load highly on multiple dimensions or because they do not load highly on any dimensions. The factor loadings for each item should be examined to determine whether it should be kept.

Conducting Reliability and Validity Analyses

Once the dimensions of the service quality survey have been determined, reliability and validity analyses can be conducted. First, coefficients alpha (the most frequently used indicator of internal homogeneity for a set of items) can be used to determine the internal reliabilities of each of the scales. When calculating the reliabilities, each item should be examined to determine what the reliability of the scale would be if the item were dropped. Items might be dropped if doing so would substantially increase the internal reliability of the scale.

In terms of validating the service quality survey, content and criterion validation strategies might be employed. As mentioned previously, gathering the opinions of customers as to whether the survey covers the issues that it needs to can be used as content validity evidence for the survey. It is important that customers, rather than the researchers, be used for this procedure, because customers are the experts about what service issues matter from the customer's perspective. While content validity evidence should be collected to support the survey, many researchers rely on criterion validity evidence alone. Typically, the scores on the service quality scale are averaged into dimensions or into a single overall score that can then be correlated with the separate global measure of service quality. That is, the overall service quality score calculated by averaging the items of the survey together would be correlated with a single overall rating or an overall rating obtained from a separate global scale. As a point of reference, Parasuraman et al. found that their five dimensions (calculated as the average of P-E scores) explained between 57% and 71% of the variance in an overall service quality item depending on the industry sample under consideration (Parasuraman, Berry, & Zeithaml, 1991a). It is interesting to note that these percentages ranged from 72% to 86% for a study using a perceptions-only measure (Parasuraman, Zeithaml, & Berry, 1994a).

Correlations with other constructs besides overall service quality can also be used to provide criterion validity evidence for a service quality survey. For example, Parasuraman, Zeithaml, and Berry (1994a) correlated responses from the survey with items assessing whether people had had a recent problem with service and whether the problem had been adequately resolved. They found higher survey scores for those who had not experienced any problems, and—among those who had experienced a problem—for those who had had their problems successfully resolved. Babakus and Boller (1992) also correlated SERVQUAL scores with an item measuring people's satisfaction with complaint resolution.

Conclusions

The steps listed above for developing surveys are essentially those followed by Parasuraman, Zeithaml, and Berry (1985, 1988) in developing SERVQUAL, as well as by other researchers developing their own measures of service quality (Dabholkar et al., 1996). Thus it might seem somewhat redundant for every service quality researcher to engage in the rather lengthy process of developing his or her own measure of service quality. However, the only measure of service quality that has been extensively researched in the literature is SERVQUAL, and it has been subjected to a number of criticisms—including criticisms of its universal applicability. Thus we recommend using the work that has been done on SERVQUAL as a starting point for a service quality measure, but efforts should be made to ensure that it is an appropriate measure for a particular research study before using it unconditionally. The basic structure of the survey can then undergo whatever modifications are necessary to make sure that the service quality measure used is appropriate.

In considering the criticisms of SERVQUAL and its applicability, it is important to remember that many of the debates addressed in this chapter did not even exist until the SERVQUAL survey was introduced. It provided one of the first comprehensive models of service quality, and it also provided a way of measuring and testing the model. SERVQUAL provided service researchers an alternative to developing their own completely unique service quality measures for each study they conducted. Its contribution in these regards cannot be overrated.

In addition, SERVQUAL is still one of the only widely recognized measures of service quality available today. While more researchers may be developing industry-specific measures of service quality, these are fairly recent additions to the literature and none of these has become widely used. If this line of work is pursued further, service quality researchers may eventually be able to turn to the literature to find a service quality scale specific to a particular industry. However, that is not the current state of affairs, and many service quality researchers still employ SERVQUAL. Furthermore, SERVQUAL still provides these researchers with valuable results and knowledge, although it should be recognized that more insights could potentially be gained from tailoring the measure to specific organizations or industries.

Notes

1. Recall from Chapter 1 the distinction that was made between the technical outcome of a service (e.g., the meal in the restaurant, the medicine prescribed by the doctor, etc.) as opposed to the functional outcome, which refers to the delivery process (Grönroos, 1990).

2. Parasuraman et al. decided that the facets or dimensions of service quality were *separable but related* constructs, and accordingly chose to use oblique rotation in their factor analysis. This procedure creates nonindependent or correlated factors from items.

3. Combining responses across automotive repair, insurance, and financial services industries, White and Schneider (2000) found only two orthogonal factors: the items designed to measure Tangibles formed one factor, while all of the other items formed another. Studying customers of a utility company, Babakus and Boller (1992) found all positively worded SERVQUAL items to load onto a single factor rather than replicating the original factor structure. (It should be noted that revisions of SERVQUAL changed the negatively worded items to be positively worded [Parasuraman, Berry, & Zeithaml, 1991a].) Furthermore, in an extensive review of the SERVQUAL survey across four industries (banking, pest control, dry cleaning, and fast food), Cronin and Taylor's (1992) factor analysis (using oblique rotation) showed that all of the items of the survey except one loaded onto a single factor.

4. Tax and Brown (2000) provide a very complete discussion of the issues related to service recovery from both research and practice perspectives. In particular, they focus on the issue of fairness and the role that recovery procedures, interactions, and outcomes play in customer perceptions of fairness.

5. Difference scores tend to have restricted variances when one component is consistently rated higher than the other. For SERVQUAL, this would take the form of expectations almost always being rated higher than the perceived level of service—a likely occurrence, since people almost always rate what they want as higher than what they have (Wall & Payne, 1973). Under the assumption that expectations will equal or exceed perceptions, rating perceptions of service at the high end of a given rating scale leaves little room for expectations to exceed them. Thus expectations and perceptions ratings will be fairly close together, and the P-E scores will be fairly uniformly low (i.e., restricted variance).

6. This definition of service quality is found in Zeithaml (1988). The definition has been cited in numerous articles, including Bolton and Drew (1991) and Bojanic (1991).

7. Sometimes called *driver analysis*, this technique is discussed in Oliver (1997) and was employed by Parasuraman, Berry, & Zeithaml (1991a) in their refinement of SERVQUAL. Here, the goal is to establish the relative contribution of service quality dimension scores to the overall judgment of service quality.

8. Furthermore, Oliver (1997) introduced a model in which quality and satisfaction are reciprocally related. We do not detail that model here except to note that it is another plausible possibility.

9. The issues in gathering questionnaire data for evaluating customer experiences of service quality are a topic worthy of a book or two of their own! See Vavra (1997) for a comprehensive, practical, step-by-step introduction to the topic and Oliver (1997) for a more conceptual/academic approach.

10. Confirmatory factor analysis is a statistical technique whereby the researcher *a priori* identifies a factor structure for his or her data, hypothesizing how many factors underlie the data and the pattern of loadings for each factor. Typically using maximum likelihood estimation, the researcher determines how well the data fit his or her model relative to other alternative models.

11. Recall from above that the relationships might be due to a higher-order "overall" service quality factor, but it is also possible that ratings on distinct dimensions are simply highly correlated with each other. It is important to keep in mind that highly correlated dimensions can still be considered separate dimensions.

References

Babakus, E., & Boller, G. (1992). An empirical assessment of the SERVQUAL scale. *Journal of Business Research, 24,* 253–268.

Baker, J. (1986). The role of the environment in marketing services. In J. Czepiel, C. Congram, & J. Shanahan (Eds.), *The service challenge: Integrating for competitive advantage* (pp. 79–84). Chicago: American Marketing Association.

Bitner, M. J. (1992). Servicescapes: The impact of physical surroundings on customers and employees. *Journal of Marketing, 56,* 57–71.

Bitner, M. J., Booms, B., & Tetreault, M. (1990). The service encounter: Diagnosing favorable and unfavorable incidents. *Journal of Marketing, 54,* 71–84.

Bojanic, D. C. (1991). Quality measurement in professional services firms. *Journal of Professional Services Marketing, 7*(2), 27–36.

Bolton, R., & Drew, J. (1991). A multistage model of customers' assessments of service quality and value. *Journal of Consumer Research, 17,* 375–385.

Brown, T. J., Churchill, G. A., Jr., & Peter, J. P. (1993). Improving the measurement of service quality. *Journal of Retailing, 69*(1), 127–139.

Carman, J. M. (1990). Consumer perceptions of service quality: An assessment of the SERVQUAL dimensions. *Journal of Retailing, 66*(1), 33–55.

Churchill, G. A. Jr., & Suprenant, C. (1982). An investigation into the determinants of customer satisfaction. *Journal of Marketing Research, 19,* 491–504.

Coyne, K. (1989). Beyond service fads: Meaningful strategies for the real world. *Sloan Management Review, 30*(4), 69–76.

Cronin, J. J., Jr., & Taylor, T. S. (1992). Measuring service quality: An examination and extension. *Journal of Marketing, 56,* 55–68.

Cronin, J. J., Jr., & Taylor, T. S. (1994). SERVPERF versus SERVQUAL: Reconciling performance-based and perceptions-minus-expectations measurement of service quality. *Journal of Marketing, 58,* 125–131.

Dabholkar, P. A., Thorpe, D. I., & Rentz, J. O. (1996). A measure of service quality for retail stores: Scale development and validation. *Journal of the Academy of Marketing Science, 24*(1), 3–16.

Fornell, C., & Wernerfelt, B. (1987). Defensive marketing strategy by customer complaint management: A theoretical analysis. *Journal of Marketing Research, 24,* 337–346.

Fornell, C., & Wernerfelt, B. (1988). A model of customer complaint management. *Marketing Science, 7*(3), 287–298.

Garvin, D. A. (1988). *Managing quality: The strategic and competitive edge.* New York: Free Press.

Grönroos, C. (1990). *Service management and marketing: Managing the moments of truth in service competition.* Lexington, MA: Lexington Books.

Gummesson, E. (1992). Quality dimensions: What to measure in service organizations. In T. A. Swartz, D. E. Bowen, & S.W. Brown (Eds.), *Advances in services marketing and management* (pp. 177–205). Greenwich, CT: JAI.

Heskett, J. L., Sasser, W. E., Jr., & Schlesinger, L. A. (1997). *The service profit chain: How leading companies link profit and growth to loyalty, satisfaction, and value.* New York: Free Press.

Kasper, H., van Helsdingen, P., & de Vries, W., Jr. (1999). *Services marketing and management: An international perspective.* Chichester, England: Wiley.

Knutson, B., Stevens, P., Wullaert, C., Patton, M., & Yokoyama, F. (1990). LODGSERV: A service quality index for the lodging industry. *Hospitality Research Journal, 14*(2), 277–284.

Loveman, G. W. (1998). Employee satisfaction, customer loyalty and financial performance: An empirical examination of the service profit chain in retail banking. *Journal of Service Research, 1*(1), 18–31.

Mangold, W. G., & Babakus, E. (1991). Service quality: The front-stage vs. the back-stage perspective. *Journal of Services Marketing, 5*(4), 59–70.

Norman, D. A. (1988). *The psychology of everyday things.* New York: Basic.

Oliva, T., Oliver, R., & MacMillan, I. (1992). A catastrophe model for developing service satisfaction strategies. *Journal of Marketing, 56*, 83–95.

Oliver, R. (1997). *Satisfaction: A behavioral perspective on the consumer.* New York: McGraw-Hill.

Parasuraman, A., Berry, L., & Zeithaml, V. (1991a). Refinement and reassessment of the SERVQUAL scale. *Journal of Retailing, 67*(4), 420–450.

Parasuraman, A., Berry, L., & Zeithaml, V. (1991b). Understanding customer expectations of service. *Sloan Management Review, 32*(3), 39–48.

Parasuraman, A., Berry, L., & Zeithaml, V. (1993). Research note: More on improving the service quality measurement. *Journal of Retailing, 79*, 420–50.

Parasuraman, A., Zeithaml, V., & Berry, L. (1985). A conceptual model of service quality and some implications for future research. *Journal of Marketing, 49*(4), 41–50.

Parasuraman, A., Zeithaml, V., & Berry, L. (1988). SERVQUAL: A multiple-item scale for measuring consumer perceptions of service quality. *Journal of Retailing, 64*(1), 12–40.

Parasuraman, A., Zeithaml, V., & Berry, L. (1994a). Alternative scales for measuring service quality: A comparative assessment based on psychometric and diagnostic criteria. *Journal of Retailing, 70*(3), 201–230.

Parasuraman, A., Zeithaml, V., & Berry, L. (1994b). Reassessment of expectations as a comparison standard in measuring service quality: Implications for further research. *Journal of Marketing, 58*, 111–124.

Reidenbach, R. E., & Sandifer-Smallwood, B. (1990). Exploring perceptions of hospital operations by a modified SERVQUAL approach. *Journal of Health Care Marketing, 10*(4), 47–55.

Rust, R., Zahorik, A., & Keiningham, T. (1996). Return on quality (ROQ): Making service quality financially accountable. In R. Rust, A. Zahorik, & T. Keiningham (Eds.), *Readings in service marketing* (pp. 193–216). New York: HarperCollins.

Schneider, B. (1973). The perception of organizational climate: The customer's view. *Journal of Applied Psychology, 57*, 248–256.

Schneider, B. (1980, Autumn). The service organization: Climate is crucial. *Organizational Dynamics*, pp. 52–65.

Schneider, B., & Bowen, D. E. (1985). Employee and customer perceptions of service in banks: Replication and extension. *Journal of Applied Psychology, 70*, 423–433.

Schneider, B., & Bowen, D. E. (1995). *Winning the service game.* Boston, MA: Harvard Business School Press.

Stevens, P., Knutson, B., & Patton, M. (1995, April). DINESERV: A tool for measuring service quality in restaurants. *Cornell Hotel and Restaurant Administration Quarterly*, pp. 56–60.

Storbacka, J., Strandvik, T., & Grönroos, C. (1994). Managing customer relationships for profit: The dynamics of relationship quality. *International Journal of Service Industry Management, 5*, 21–28.

Sutton, R. I., & Rafaeli, A. (1988). Untangling the relationship between displayed emotions and organizational sales: The case of convenience stores. *Academy of Management Journal, 31*(3), 461–487.

Tax, S. S., & Brown, S. W. (2000). Service recovery: Research insights and practice. In T. A. Swartz & D. Iacobucci (Eds.), *Handbook of services marketing and management* (pp. 271–285). Thousand Oaks, CA: Sage.

Teas, R. K. (1993). Expectations, performance evaluation, and consumers' perceptions of quality. *Journal of Marketing, 57*, 18–34.

Vavra, T. G. (1997). *Improving your measurement of customer satisfaction.* Milwaukee, WI: ASQ Quality.

Wall, T., & Payne, R. (1973). Are deficiency scores deficient? *Journal of Applied Psychology, 58*(3), 322–326.

White, S., & Schneider, B. (2000). Climbing the advocacy ladder: The impact of disconfirmation of service expectations on customers' behavioral intentions. *Journal of Services Research, 2*(3), 240–253.

Woodside, A. G., Frey, L. L., & Daly, R. T. (1989). Linking service quality, customer satisfaction, and behavioral intention. *Journal of Health Care Marketing, 9,* 5–17.

Zeithaml, V. (1988). Consumer perceptions of price, quality, and value: A means-end model and synthesis of evidence. *Journal of Marketing, 52,* 2–22.

Zeithaml, V., Berry, L., & Parasuraman, A. (1993). The nature and determinants of customer expectations of service. *Journal of the Academy of Marketing Science, 21*(1), 1–12.

Zeithaml, V., & Bitner, M. J. (2000). *Services marketing: Integrating customer focus across the firm* (2nd ed.). Boston, MA: McGraw-Hill.

Zeithaml, V., Parasuraman, A., & Berry, L. L. (1990). *Delivering quality service.* New York: Free Press.

3 Service Operations and the Presence of the Customer

I n the previous chapter, we focused on what the customer experiences in interactions with the service firm. In the next few chapters, we change our focus to *how* the firm delivers the service experienced by those customers. That is, we examine in more detail what the firm does (i.e., how it behaves) to yield the experiences that customers have. In the current chapter, we will address issues surrounding the design of service delivery *processes,* where those processes have been traditionally conceptualized from the vantage point of operations management (OM).

Thus the current chapter is intended to provide an OM perspective on service, and we will see how OM researchers have thought about customers and their role in the service delivery process. Of course, in the realm of services, it is difficult to isolate delivery *processes* from the *systems* in which they exist, the *employees* who carry them out, and the *customers* that they are designed to serve. The interrelationships among these pieces have emerged as their own topic of study—one that we will address a bit here and in more detail in Chapters 4 and 5.

OM has its roots in the manufacturing sector, where its central concerns have been to improve the effectiveness and efficiency of production with a focus on reducing variability both in inputs to production and the outputs of production. This focus on reducing variability on inputs in particular becomes a central issue for OM when we switch to service production, because service production frequently involves dealing with highly variable inputs—diversity in the customers requiring the production and delivery of a service. As you will see, this concern for variability in the inputs to the service delivery production process has effectively been reduced to a focus on the *management* of variability, since the people who come to service facilities for service are frequently so variable! As Fitzimmons and Fitzimmons (1994) put it:

For services, the process is the product. The presence of the customer in the service process negates the closed-system perspective taken in manufacturing. . . . Techniques to control operations in an isolated factory producing a tangible good are inadequate for services. In services it is the human element that is central to effective operations. For example, unavoidable interaction between service and consumer is a source of great opportunity. However, this interaction can seldom be fully controlled; thus service quality may suffer. (pp. 32–33)

Recall from Chapter 1 that heterogeneity is a defining characteristic of services: Each customer who appears for service is unique. Because customers are present for—and often even involved in—the production of their own services, the variability in customers as inputs necessarily translates into variability in service production, while the production process still maintains a concern for efficiency and effectiveness in terms of customer experiences. Given this customer variability and resultant service heterogeneity, OM scholars have had to face the challenge of designing service delivery processes that will yield quality delivery despite the presence and/or involvement of highly variable customers in production. The special genius of the OM perspective on service quality has been to integrate customers, in all of their complexity and variability, into service production processes.

As we view the history of the idea of customer contact through the OM lens, we will also introduce useful ideas concerning optimization models, quality-cost tradeoffs, and revenue management. Optimization models and quality-cost tradeoffs refer to ways to assess the customer satisfaction and revenue consequences of introducing enhanced service quality for customers. It turns out that it may not pay to have service at the highest levels possible; middling service may do just fine given market characteristics and revenue projections. Revenue management is another way to frame profit issues in services. In its simplest form, revenue management asks the following question: "Given limited capacity (as in a hotel or as in an airplane), how can I maximize the revenue generated?" Service facilities frequently have limited capacities—hotels have only so many rooms per night, airplanes have only so many seats per flight—so the challenge is to fill as many rooms and seats as possible for a given night or a given flight *for the maximum revenue.* Thus, as we noted in Chapter 1, another defining characteristic of services is perishability—that some service opportunities for customers exist only once and cannot be inventoried. Perishability for services can stand in stark contrast to perishability for goods, which can be set aside (i.e., inventoried) for consumption at another time and place. It is tough to inventory hotel rooms or airplane seats.

We go into detail on these issues for several reasons. First, the decisions made about how to handle these operational issues naturally have implications for the larger organization in which the decisions are implemented. For example, with regard to demand and capacity, whether a food-service delivery system is designed as a cafeteria or as a linen tablecloth facility has obvious implications for the atmosphere created in the facility, the price charged for the food, the kinds of people hired and the training they will receive, the role of the customer in production of their own services, and so forth. Fitzimmons and Fitzimmons (1994) noted that "the full utilization of service capacity becomes a management challenge because customer demand exhibits considerable variation, and unlike the situation in manufacturing, building inventory to absorb the fluctuation is not an option" (p. 28). So, not only do customers individually vary from each other, but they collectively vary in when service must be delivered to them. The issue is how to delivery consistent quality in the face of this variability.

Whenever the issue of quality is raised, the work described in Chapter 1 on the emergence of the quality movement (e.g., the work of Deming and Juran) automatically comes back into focus. That work was basically designed to produce consistent quality by eliminating variability in input to manufacturing, in manufacturing processes, and in output from manufacturing. One eliminates variability in manufacturing by ensuring that production processes, from the materials entering the process through the processes to the output, reach the tightest tolerances; variability is to be eliminated. But if service delivery processes involve customers and customers are inherently variable, how can quality be achieved? Scholars interested in OM have wrestled quite effectively with this issue, and we will explore some of that wrestling here.

In summary, we note that the OM focus of this chapter is dictated by the challenge to design service delivery production processes that will yield quality delivery given the fact that customers are not only present for, but also frequently participate in, production. The special genius of the OM perspective on service quality is that the customer, in all of his or her complexity and variability, is introduced as such an integral part of the process.

The Customer-Contact Model of Service Delivery

Richard Chase and his colleagues (Chase, 1978, 1981; Chase & Tansik, 1983) were among the first of the OM field to introduce the idea that the customer had to be included in thinking about the design of service delivery processes. Specifically, Chase and Tansik (1983) proposed a normative model of operating efficiency in service production across industries that included customers, holding that customer contact in organizations was a factor in determining operating efficiency:

$$\text{Potential Operating Efficiency} = f\left(1 - \frac{\text{Customer Contact Time}}{\text{Service Creating Time}}\right)$$

According to the model, efficiency decreases as a greater proportion of the time spent creating the service is spent in contact with the customer. Thus operating efficiency will be superior to the extent that processes can be designed to limit the amount of time spent in contact with the customer during service production. In a manufacturing context, processes could be designed to reduce the level of customer contact time to approximately zero, and operating efficiency would be high. For services, as we have noted several times, customers are frequently present for service production and they are sometimes involved in the production of the services they receive. The highly variable ways in which customers behave during this contact time in turn reduces the consistency with which service delivery processes can be applied— which in turn reduces the efficiency of operations.

Chase (1981) was perfectly clear about the implications of the customer-contact model (p. 703). He first proposed that firms should reduce customer contact whenever feasible to improve efficiency. For example, the backroom production issues associated with mortgage banks might be moved to a central location for efficiency purposes. Then, firms should apply traditional efficiency improvement techniques (e.g., statistical quality control) to their work. However, it may not always be possible to remove customer contact altogether. When it is necessary, firms should employ contact enhancement strategies. Here, Chase presents the example of Benihana of Tokyo restaurants. Saddled with high costs due to central city locations, Benihana made dining into a high-customer-contact service with flamboyant chefs producing a "show" at each table—thus achieving the efficiency goal of not needing a large kitchen.

Given the implications of customer contact for the design of processes to achieve efficiency, OM scholars have devoted some attention to getting a handle on just how much customer contact the delivery of a particular service will involve. Chase (1978) and Chase and Aquilano (1977) described three types of services based on the degree

Table 3.1   Classification of Service Systems Based on Customer Contact

Contact Low → High			
"Pure" Service	*"Mixed" Service*	*Quasi-Manufacturing*	*Manufacturing*
Health centers	Branch offices of bank	Home offices of bank	Durables
Hotels			
Public transport	Computer firms	Computer firms	Food processing
Restaurants	Real estate	Government admin.	Mining
Schools	Post offices	Wholesale houses	Chemicals
Personal services	Funeral homes	Post offices	Etc.
Freedom in Designing Efficient Production Procedures Low → High			

SOURCE: From Chase, Northcraft, and Wolf (1984). "Designing high contact service systems: Application to branches of a savings and loan," in *Decision Sciences, 15.* Reprinted with permission.

of customer contact involved: pure services, mixed services, and quasi-manufacturing. Table 3.1 summarizes these ideas in some detail (Chase 1978; Chase, Northcraft, & Wolf, 1984).

Pure services obviously involve the highest degree of customer contact, as these are the types of services produced in the presence of the customer (e.g., medical care, cafeteria food service). Mixed services involve both face-to-face components and backroom components (e.g., branch banks), while quasi-manufacturing involves no face-to-face contact (e.g., automatic teller machines). A fourth category of "manufacturing" describes products with no service component.

Most importantly, Table 3.1 and the customer-contact perspective make the point that not all services are created equal. Accordingly, not all service delivery processes need to be the same. Certain features of delivery may be more important for a high-contact service than a low-contact one, capacity issues may become more or less manageable, and so forth. Chase and Tansik (1983) captured their ideas of the issues associated with customer contact in several explicit propositions *when high contact characterizes the service on which one is focused* (p. 1042). These propositions, a summary of which is presented in Table 3.2, highlight the (relative) presence of the customer as a contingency variable affecting service process delivery decisions and designs.

Table 3.2   OM Characteristics of High-Contact Services—Some Propositions

1. The service product is multidimensional (time, place, atmosphere) and hence its quality is in the eye of the beholder.
2. The direct worker is part of the service product.
3. Demand for the service is often instantaneous and hence cannot be stored.
4. Because production is generally customer initiated, an optimal balance between service system demand and resources is difficult to achieve.
5. Changes in the capacity of the system affect the nature of the service product.
6. The production schedule has a direct, personal effect on the consumer.
7. Only part of the service can be kept in inventory.
8. Verbal skills and knowledge of policy are usually required of the service worker.
9. Wage payments must usually be related to labor hours spent rather than output.
10. It is assumed that service system capacity is at its long-run level when the system first opens.
11. A service system malfunction will have an immediate, direct effect on the customer.
12. The location of the service system modifies its value to the customer.

SOURCE: Reprinted by permission. Chase, R. B. "The customer contact approach to services: Theoretical bases and practical extensions," in *Operations Research, 29(4).* Copyright © 1981, the Institute for Operations Research and the Management Sciences (INFORMS), 901 Elkridge Landing Road, Suite 400, Linthicum, Maryland 21090-2909 USA.

The propositions take a healthy open-system view of all of the issues we have discussed to this point: the presence/participation of the customer, the role of human resources management (HRM) and/or organizational behavior (OB), demand/capacity issues, perishability of the service, the fact that service quality is in the eye of the beholder (a topic addressed in Chapter 2), and so forth. These early propositions of the high-customer-contact model received great attention for two reasons. First, they were useful in that they could be relatively easily attended to once they were identified. This was especially true because one of the earliest versions of the model (Chase, 1978) appeared in the *Harvard Business Review.* As such, it received immediate attention from managers and executives who might not have been aware of it had it appeared in *Management Science* or *Operations Science.* Second, the customer-contact model illuminated issues that were of concern beyond OM. That is, there were propositions of interest to those dealing with compensation issues (Proposition 9, concerning wages for workers), to those dealing with hiring and training issues (Proposition 8, concerning knowledge and skill requirements for workers), and so forth (see Table 3.2).

This point about the systems view of the high-contact service delivery firm is important, because the OM approach has been characterized by what is called an open-systems model of organizational functioning. Loosely defined, an open-systems model is one that includes both the larger environment in which the firm operates as well as relationships among the internal parts of the organization. Those interested in service quality, regardless of whether they identify most strongly with marketing, OM, or HRM/OB, seem implicitly to understand that it is the interrelationships among these three facets of the organization that make for effective service delivery vis-à-vis the external customer.

Indeed, the neat and relatively straightforward conceptualization presented in the early 1980s became so well accepted that little empirical research was actually conducted on it. It was not until 1995 that an actual measure of customer contact was developed so that the features of high- and low-contact service facilities could be identified (Kellogg & Chase, 1995). Research on other features of service delivery emerging from the customer-contact conceptualization did take place, and we will review this work later. For now, we note that Chase's framework was not the only one that was developed relevant to (a) customer contact and (b) service design and delivery. In the next section, we discuss the more elaborate framework proposed by Lovelock (1983), and we will then present research relevant to the Chase and Lovelock models.

Classification of Services by Lovelock

In 1983, Lovelock proposed a classification scheme for services for the main purpose of aiding marketers in designing strategic marketing programs. However, the model is easily applicable to any use—just as Chase's model is useful for HRM and marketing as well as OM. In Lovelock's model, services are classified by their placement along two dimensions: (1) Who or what is the direct recipient of the service? and (2) What is the nature of the service act? With regards to the first question, Lovelock held that the recipients of the service can be either *people* (as would be the case for health care, restaurants, etc.) or *things* (as would be the case for janitorial services, auto repair, etc.). With regards to the second question, Lovelock describes service acts as either *tangible*, like a haircut or a meal in a restaurant, or *intangible*, like broadcasting or legal services. Readers will recall our earlier discussion of intangibility as an attribute of services, and those same ideas apply here. Lovelock's point, like the one made earlier by Chase (1981), is of course that all services are not created equal.

Table 3.3   Understanding the Nature of the Service Act

		Who or what is the direct recipient of the service?	
		People	*Things*
What is the nature of the service act?	*Tangible*	Services directed at people's bodies Health care Passenger transportation Beauty salons Exercise clinics Restaurants	Services directed at goods Freight transportation Industrial equipment repair Janitorial services Laundry and dry cleaning Landscaping/lawn care
	Intangible	Services directed at people's minds Education Broadcasting Information services Theaters Museums	Services directed at intangible assets Banking Legal Services Accounting Securities Insurance

SOURCE: Adapted from Lovelock (1983). "Classifying services to gain strategic marketing insights," *Journal of Marketing, 47,* pp. 9-20. Copyright © 1983 by American Marketing Association. Used with permission.

Lovelock conceptualized "service acts" as falling somewhere in the 2 x 2 table created by the people/things and tangible/intangible dimensions. An example of one of Lovelock's 2 x 2 tables is shown in Table 3.3. Lovelock was concerned with more than customer contact as a key issue, but customer contact is the first issue he addressed in his original framework and more recent versions of the framework put the customer central. In fact, what Lovelock is concerned with are *processes,* what he calls "service acts." While the models were developed for marketing, the OM perspective on them is that service delivery processes will vary depending on where in this 2 x 2 table the service act lies.

Lovelock (1983) suggested that different classifications of service acts would yield different answers to the following questions:

a. Does the customer need to be *physically* present
  • throughout service delivery?
  • only to initiate or terminate the service transaction (e.g., dropping off a car for repair)?

- not at all (e.g., their relationship with the service supplier can be at arm's length through the mail, telephone, or other electronic media)?
 b. Does the customer need to be *mentally* present during the service delivery? Can mental presence be maintained across physical distances through mail or electronic communications? (pp. 12–13)

The answers to these questions would obviously vary depending on where in Lovelock's 2 x 2 table the service act under consideration falls, and the answers have implications for the design of service delivery processes. Reminiscent of Chase's thinking, Lovelock held that efficiency would best be achieved through processes that eliminated the presence of the customer—by creating what Lovelock called a "service factory" (or what Chase called his low-contact model). He stated that "for operational reasons it may be very desirable to get the customer out of the factory and to transform a 'high contact' service into a 'low contact' one" (Lovelock, 1983, p. 14). Even in 1983, he was able to cite several creative ways that service firms could put the customer at arm's length: ATMs, pay-by-phone bill paying, and education via television broadcasting, for example.

In this groundbreaking paper, Lovelock created a series of 2 x 2 figures like Table 3.3, although we present only that one here. Other figures concern where services fall on other dimensions:

1. *The customer-service firm relationship:* Is the customer a member (e.g., telephone, banking) or is there no formal relationship to the firm (e.g., radio station, police protection)?
 a. *Customization:* Is the service delivered highly customized for each customer (legal services) or virtually the same for each customer (e.g., fast-food restaurants)?
 b. *Demand fluctuation:* To what degree does customer demand for services fluctuate over time (hour, day, week, season)? For example, demands for electricity increase in summer when air conditioners are in use. Insurance companies, such as the United Services Automobile Association (USAA), sometimes ask policyholders not to call on Mondays (except in an emergency), because Mondays are the busiest days of the week. Hotels offer lower weekend rates because the lack of business travelers lowers demand. (This is an issue we will address in more detail later when we discuss yield management, a tactic for dealing with fluctuating demand-supply relationships.)

It is difficult to overemphasize the insights that Lovelock presented in this paper. Recall that the idea of service delivery as something special was not even a decade old when his paper was published. And, though Lovelock published it as a paper yielding insights into the *marketing* of services, the paper was really about tactics for delivering services that took into account the customer—the article was about service *processes*. In fact, Lovelock has recently (2001) reflected on the 1983 paper this way: "I continue to believe that the most fundamental classification of services pertains to the nature of the underlying *processes . . .*" (p. 134). More than that, however, Lovelock's classification—like Chase's—was really about *customer involvement in processes*.

Lovelock's presentation confronted researchers and practitioners alike with the idea that customers had to be taken into account when thinking about service delivery. Of course this does not mean that researchers and practitioners actually *did* this. As we proceed with the next section of the chapter, it will become clearer why the customer should be considered in the internal world of the service organization.

Potential Benefits of Customer Coproduction

The title of this section should not be interpreted to mean (a) that all service production requires customer participation, (b) that it is always a good idea to involve customers in service production, or (c) that we think companies can improve revenues, profits, and customer loyalty by involving customers in production. What the title means is that there are some circumstances under which customer participation in production, especially when customers are already present for production, can be beneficial. Customer participation can be beneficial because of cost savings and/or increased commitment on the part of the customer. Cost savings obviously would be due to a need for fewer employees, as in a fast-food restaurant where customers act both as wait staff and as bussers of their tables. Commitment on the part of the customer might be due to the effort extended by customers in production as a result of the rule that effort breeds commitment to the effort (Salancik, 1977).

The models developed by Chase and Lovelock encouraged the *consideration* of the customer's role in production, asking the following question: If customers are present, why not have them help? This approach is much more positive vantage point on the customer than simply regarding customers as a problem—a drain on efficiency. As Zeithaml and Bitner (2000) point out, there are a variety of ways in which customers can serve as coproducers: helping themselves, helping others, and promoting the company, with these many ways each potentially contributing to the bottom line. Lovelock and Young (1979) were perhaps the first to develop the notion that service organizations might actually improve productivity by essentially thinking of customers as partial employees in the production of their own services.

Involving customers in the production of their own services is, of course, only one option for improving service delivery in high-customer-contact firms. Another option, and one we will discuss later, is to change the timing of customer demand; this is the issue of managing demand we noted earlier. Of course, the organization might also increase the use of technology, increase the available staff, enlarge the service facility, and so on. Indeed, Lengnick-Hall (1996) noted that a failure to capitalize on customer involvement in services production is very similar to the model of management that assumes employees lack creativity, initiative, and talent. She sees the potential for the involvement of customers in service production from a broader vantage point than did Lovelock and Young: Customers should be treated like adults who are capable, desire to participate, and will derive satisfaction from a job well done.

The unique proposal of Lovelock and Young (1979) was to use customers themselves as a vehicle for improving production efficiency mostly through cost reductions associated with decreased need for employees. In this seminal article, Lovelock and Young provide several early examples of how organizations profited by designing their processes to involve customers in production. For example, in the late 1960s, AT&T introduced the use of direct long-distance dialing. Although it took time and extensive marketing efforts to get the population to place their own long-distance calls, 75% of all long-distance calls were direct dialed by 1973—with labor savings of $37 million per year. Other less extreme examples include having coffee makers in hotel rooms so that guests can make their own coffee, having customers bus their own tables in fast-food restaurants, or, more recently, self-scanning of items at the supermarket ("Do It Yourself," 1994). There is some research to show that customer participation can pay in ways other than savings in employee salaries. For example, research shows that in self-service gas stations there is increased revenue from increased sales of beer, soda, snacks, and other store items (Solomon, 1993).

Of course, not all customers want to participate in their own services production (Zeithaml & Bitner, 2000), something we've known for quite a long time (Bateson, 1983). Lovelock (2001) goes one step further and presents a listing of the customer as potential hindrance to production. He calls such customers "jaycustomers," and defines them as follows: "Jaycustomers are undesirable. At worst a firm needs to control or prevent their abusive behavior. At best it would like to avoid attracting them in the first place" (p. 73). These jaycustomers fall into six main categories: the thief, the rule breaker, the belligerent, the family feuder (who gets into arguments with others, including family members), the vandal (who beats up on the service facility itself), and the deadbeat. Empirical data on the frequency of these behaviors by customers and the costs associated with them could prove useful, but to our knowledge there is no published research on these issues.

Furthermore, we are unaware of research on the loyalty or commitment of customers to the service firm as a function of their level of participation in production. As noted earlier, such commitment should be the result of effort in production. Orsingher (1999) explored the degree to which customers who are aware of the roles (or *scripts*) they must play as customers experience higher levels of satisfaction and loyalty in a study conducted in Italy, but we are not aware of other such research. And Cermak, File, and Prince (1994) showed that effort expended in participation as a customer resulted in increased intentions to purchase in the future. The antecedents and consequences of customer participation in production could be an interesting area of both conceptual and practical usefulness, especially if the work is approached from the vantage point of OB/HRM, as Schneider and Bowen (1995) suggest. In brief, they recommend that when customers will be used as coproducers, a careful job analysis be conducted of the role, assess customer expectations/knowledge for their role, train them if necessary, motivate customers by rewarding their effort and ensuring they enjoy participation, and appraise customer performance to ensure they continue to contribute as planned (see also Lengnick-Hall, 1996).

Managing Variability Through a Focus on the Customer

Of course, putting a positive spin on the presence of the customer through coproduction does not eliminate the variability that customers bring to the production process. Processes that involve customer participation necessarily introduce variability in input—the bane of quality production, as we discussed in Chapter 1. The focus must then turn to managing variability in service delivery—because it cannot be eliminated. For example, in discussing recent health care trends, McLaughlin (1996) holds that it is necessary for health care providers to eliminate variation in service delivery where they can as "the ultimate objective of delivering health care *with its inherent variability* [italics added] in a mass customization mode" (p. 17).[1]

One procedure with the goal of reducing variability is based on processes developed by Shigeo Shingo, the man who created such process innovations as Just-in-Time manufacturing at Toyota Motors (Chase & Stewart, 1994). The unique perspective of Shingo was that one need not wait for a defect to occur to implement procedures. He proposed that the way to prevent defects was to "fail-safe" the manufacturing process.

Chase and Stewart (1994) applied Shingo's notion to the service sector, and considered the role of the customer to fail-safe the service delivery process. That is, they planned for the variability in services production associated with customer involvement. Chase and Stewart proposed that three aspects of customer participation must be addressed to fail-safe service delivery: (1) preparation for the customer encounter, (2) the customer encounter itself, and (3) resolution of the encounter.

Preparing the customer for the encounter is frequently overlooked as a tactic in reducing customer variability, but it can be an important step in efforts to approach uniformity in service delivery. Customers do not usually have prior information about what their roles are or should be, or what knowledge, paperwork or other tangibles they must bring to the encounter. In other words, customers are often unaware of the requirements for an encounter, so they do not prepare. Differences in preparation in turn yield differences in service delivery.

During the encounter, customers can be unaware of how to behave—what to do upon arrival, where to proceed upon arrival, how to signal the need for help, and so forth. For example, one of us once ate in a cafeteria where the process of service delivery called on customers to raise a small flag at their table if they needed assistance. However, the meaning of these flags was anything but obvious, and differences in the usage of the flags introduced unnecessary variability into the delivery of service. Finally, in the postencounter phase, we have an opportunity to evaluate the encounter itself and derive bases for action from these assessments. That is, lessons learned from customers in the postencounter phase of service delivery can be used to help reduce variability in future encounters.

In further efforts to conceptualize how service organizations can address customer variability, Lengnick-Hall (1996) argued that organizations should actively establish routines and behaviors for customers to follow at the pre-encounter, encounter, or postencounter phase, yielding improved (i.e., less variable) input into production. Indeed, Lengnick-Hall, like Schneider and Bowen (1995), proposed that service firms literally select, train, and motivate customers so that they can effectively play service production roles. More specifically, Lengnick-Hall's conceptualizes the coproducing customer not only as (a) an input or resource in production, but also as (b) a user, buyer, and product of production as well. As users of the service that has been produced, customers are invaluable as feedback mechanisms for organizations. A service firm (or any firm, for that matter) can benefit from having complete information on how customers experience what they buy—if they take advantage of such information to improve their service. Acting on such user information can have considerable competitive advantage (Garvin, 1988; Schneider & Bowen, 1995). As buyers of the service produced, customers who are viewed as resources and are included in the production of a service might be expected to develop deeper relationships with the firm—and to keep buying services from that firm in the future!

Bitner, Faranda, Hubbert, and Zeithaml (1997) present a framework for understanding customer participation in production that is quite similar to the one presented by Lengnick-Hall (1996). What Bitner et al. add, however, is some empirical research on their framework.[2] This is especially important given how little research has actually been conducted on customer participation in production.

Harking back to the Chase and Lovelock models of customer contact, a basic feature of the Bitner et al. (1997) framework is that services differ in levels of customer participation in production. They describe a project with Weight Watchers International, where the main service is losing weight—a service that obviously cannot be produced without high customer participation. What was really interesting in their study was the finding that, in examining customer satisfaction, results showed that weight loss was only one determinant of satisfaction with Weight Watchers. The other determinants of customer satisfaction all had to do with customer-contact issues: Procedures, information, knowledge, empathy, and support provided by Weight Watchers also affected satisfaction, *regardless of the weight lost.* That is, the customer-contact delivery procedures as well as the outcomes influenced satisfaction with the high-involvement service.

This discussion of the role of the customer in service production has lent us some understanding of the variability that customers introduce into the production of services and how this seemingly inherent variability can be somewhat reduced by taking prior action to reduce variability through information, prior previews, and so forth. Of course, there are also ways to reduce service production variability without introducing the issue of the customer at all. As students of OB, we seem to always want to introduce *people* into the equation, whether those people be employees as service deliverers or customers as coproducers and service recipients. Given this predilection to want to focus on people, it is instructive to consider ways OM scholars have found to reduce variability in quality without any attention to people.

Reducing Variability Through a Focus on the Facility

Although some variability in the production of services will always exist, reducing it can have numerous potential long-term benefits. In particular, it is useful to eliminate the variability that is responsible for causing problems. This type of variability is the focus of root cause analysis (RCA). RCA is a set of procedures designed originally for solving manufacturing problems, but it is now being applied in service delivery systems (Dorsch, Yasin, & Czuchry, 1997). The fundamental idea behind RCA is *not* to pay attention to symptoms, but rather to pay attention to fundamental causes—or roots—of identified problems.

Dorsch et al. (1997) provide an excellent example of RCA applied to services in their paper concerning hotel carpets that are continuously found to be dirty and dusty. As OB researchers, we might first ask whether some staff are failing to vacuum. In fact, data show there is variability among cleaning crews in the cleanliness of carpets. It could therefore be easily concluded that this is a personnel issue (poor training, poor motivation, etc.). But wait! It turns out that the crews who get the carpets clean are actually cleaning a different kind of carpet than the crews that are leaving the carpets dirty. The root cause of dirty carpets is the use of the same kind of vacuum cleaner for the different kinds of carpets. This example illustrates the value of delving into issues to get to their root causes.

Dorsch et al. (1997) suggest that a reason why companies fail to get at the root of problems they identify, even when they use RCA, is that they approach problem solving from a specific vantage point. For example, HRM people find the root cause in people, OM people find the root cause in delivery processes, and marketing people find the root cause in customer expectations. Dorsch et al. propose that all RCAs include exploration of all of these potential causes prior to reaching a conclusion. We will return later in the book to this notion of using multiple vantage points to understand service quality. For now, we simply note that Dorsch et al. proposed that all RCA analyses include exploration of procedures, personnel, equipment, materials, and the environment as the potential root causes of identified problems.

Linking Operational Procedures to Service Quality and Profits, Too

Certainly, a major reason for focusing on service delivery processes, including the role of the customer in them, is ultimately to design processes that will be profitable. There are, of course, many routes to profits in business. The marketing perspective proposes that exceeding expectations yields customer delight and repeat business which, eventually, improves profits. The HRM/OB perspective, the topic of Chapter 4, proposes that the key to profits is to have effective human resources management. A significant facet of the OM approach to profits is to put in place effective service delivery procedures at costs that are lower than existing procedures.

An excellent example of a model linking service delivery processes to costs has recently been presented by Soteriou and Chase (in press). The authors not only address the issue of whether there is a link between service delivery processes and customer perceptions of service quality, they also examine the processes in terms of the costs associated with them. They develop a robust optimization framework for simultaneously taking into account the cost of processes and the relationship of the processes to customer experiences of service quality.

The authors collected data at an outpatient clinic of a large medical center; the clinic had more than 3,000 visits per month with patients of medium to low socioeconomic background. Data were gathered on the following operational variables: employee training, waiting time, incident duration, cleaning frequency of the incident area, and cleaning frequency of the bathroom in the waiting area serving the incident. Customers completed the SERVPERF measure of service quality (described in Chapter 2) in either English or Spanish (Cronin & Taylor, 1992, 1994). The authors' analyses attempted to demonstrate relationships between the patients' perceptions of service quality with the operational variables described above.[3]

In terms of results, there were actually more significant linkages between service quality perceptions and the operational variables than had been expected. Training was related to perceptions of service quality, and frequency of cleaning the incident areas also revealed significant links with facets of service quality. Of additional interest in the models that were developed were the attributes of the customers themselves and of the treating staff. For example, the presenting symptom of patients was correlated with the service quality facet of Responsiveness, with sicker patients reporting more Responsiveness in the examination stage. With regard to the staff providing treatment, there seemed to be no effect for whether treatment was by a physician, a nurse, a physician assistant, or a nurse practitioner.

Once these linkages were established, the second set of questions regarding combining the factors could be raised. To start, what combination of the set of operational predictor variables (e.g., training, cleaning, etc.) is required to achieve a target level of service quality? In the present case, results revealed that management could improve service quality perceptions from 5.09 to 5.92 on a 7-point scale by doubling the current amount spent on training, by increasing staffing levels from 13 to 18 (with all of that in nurses), and doubling the frequency of cleaning the bathroom that served the area in which the patient was examined and treated.

Next, Soteriou and Chase (in press) asked a second question: Given a level of service quality, what is the best combination of predictor variables for achieving that target level at the lowest *cost?* They found that the optimal solution was to (1) increase the number of personnel in the examination area, (2) decrease the number of personnel in the financial area, and (3) encourage voluntary training (a specific kind of employee training) more so than had been done in the past.

The Soteriou and Chase (in press) research is not rare, with many examples of this tradeoff being of interest. What is rare is the application of this kind of thinking to service delivery. As Lovelock (2001) puts it

> It's usually harder for managers to calculate the financial costs involved in creating an intangible performance for a customer than it is to identify the labor, materials, machine time, storage, and shipping costs associated with producing a physical good whose ownership is transferred to the customer upon purchase. (p. 259)

Rust and his colleagues (Rust, Zahorik, & Keiningham, 1995; Zahorik, Rust, & Keiningham, 2000) have proposed that there are two major issues to consider when thinking about service processes and costs to improve service quality: (1) What are the costs of failure to improve quality? and (2) What are the costs associated with improving service quality compared to the benefits thereof? Rust and his colleagues persuasively argue that the issue here is to ensure that investments in service quality enhancements (a) address areas where poor service quality is costing the company (in the form of defections, costs to correct problems, and so forth) and (b) provide enhancements in service quality that are the most beneficial in terms of cost-benefit analysis. With regard to this second point, Lovelock (2001) summarizes the Rust et al. approach this way:

> Rust and his colleagues argue for a Return on Quality (ROQ) approach based on the assumptions that (1) quality is an investment, (2) quality efforts must be financially accountable, (3) it's possible to spend too much on quality, and (4) not all quality expenditures are equally valid. (p. 375)

Obviously, a key to Rust et al.'s ROQ approach is to know the following linkages (see the Appendix to Chapter 14 in Rust, Zahorik, and Keiningham, 1996, for more details):

1. *The Customer Satisfaction (with specific facets of service)–Customer Retention Link:* If satisfaction is not strongly related to retention, then it may not be financially useful to invest in service quality enhancements that produce customer satisfaction. It is very important to understand that the importance of satisfaction with a specific facet of service quality is determined by its linkage (correlation) to retention, not someone's (manager's, customer's) *opinion* about what is important.

2. *Customer Retention–Market Share Link:* The critical issue here is the number of current customers who will be retained and the number of new customers attracted to the firm if the firm does nothing in the way of improvements. In its starkest terms, it may not pay to invest in service quality improvements if the business will grow and retain its customers by doing nothing different. However, if the firm can increase its market share by retaining a larger number of current customers, then it may be worth the investments to yield greater retention.

3. *Market Share–Revenues Link:* This is usually straightforward, but it requires such information as the average profit per customer and the size of the market.

Data on these linkages must next be combined with knowledge of what it will cost to take the various steps for improving customer satisfaction. This will put the firm in a position to estimate the effects of an improvement on customer satisfaction, the effect of customer retention on market share, and the effects of market share on revenues. By looking at these together with the costs associated with making the changes, the firm can determine the benefits of making the changes.

One need not go to the extremes of the Rust et al. procedure to find a linkage between operational procedures and profitability. For example, Kimes (1999) has carefully documented the importance of attention to operational details in hotels. More specifically, she studied 1,135 franchised Holiday Inn hotels over a three-year period and examined the consequences of poor quality in terms of revenues per available room per day (RPRPD). Kimes obtained operational data from quality assurance inspections done at the hotels by Holiday Inn inspectors. Hotels were coded as defective or effective in the following operational areas: lobby, public restrooms, dining, lounge, corridors, recreation, meeting, kitchen, exterior, back of house, guest room, and guest bath. She found that hotels with defects in certain areas had lower RPRPD levels than hotels that were effective in those areas—and that the decrement in RPRPD differed depending on the defective area under consideration. A defect on the exterior was associated with $3.12 less in RPRPD, a defect in a guest room was associated with $2.01 less in RPRPD, and a defect in a guest bath was associated with $1.32 less in RPRPD. When hotels were coded as being overall defective, they had $2.80 less in RPRPD than hotels coded nondefective. While $2.80 RPRPD may seem small, the annual impact of this differential is $204,400 per year per hotel![4]

In considering these studies of operational issues, it is interesting to recall that we began this chapter with a discussion of the importance of customer contact in thinking about the application of quality improvement tactics to service firms. Yet, in the studies we just reviewed, the presence of the customer is not central in estimating the returns that can be expected from investments in quality. One reason behind this may be the lack of empirical research on customer contact: It is difficult to incorporate customer contact into these models without numbers to associate with the concept. That is, in the absence of research on the operationalization of customer contact, it has been difficult to introduce customer contact as a variable in optimization and ROQ models.

One effort to research the concept of customer contact was conducted by Kellogg and Chase (1995), who empirically derived a measurement model for customer contact. Their research involved having observers rate videotaped reenactments of 13 episodes that had actually taken place in a hospital setting. The episodes were chosen to represent varying degrees of customer contact (based on *a priori* estimates), according to the central measurement principle that variability in the phenomenon of interest must exist to correlate it with another variable. Through various analytic techniques, including multidimensional scaling and regression analysis, the authors found that the observers distinguished among the episodes in terms of customer contact. The episodes ranged in customer contact from dietary workers (with no customer contact), through admissions (with moderate customer contact), to registered nurses (with high customer contact). The authors' results also revealed that three predictors explained almost all of the variation in customer contact and can thus be considered keys to understanding what customer contact means. These three predictors were Communication Time, Information Richness, and Intimacy.[5] These are defined below:

> *Communication Time:* the number of seconds involved in communicating.
>
> *Information Richness:* a composite indicator made up of the use of both audio and visual channels of communication, the use of both verbal and nonverbal (body) language, and the immediacy of feedback between the service worker and the customer.
>
> *Intimacy:* the degree to which the episode could be described as mutual and confiding in trust.

In a follow-up to this Kellogg and Chase (1995) paper, Soteriou and Chase (1998) asked the following question: Is there a relationship between customer contact and service quality? Two dimensions of customer contact—Communication Time (Time) and Intimacy—were studied, and service quality was operationalized by the five dimensions of SERVQUAL (see Chapter 2). The study involved clocking the amount of time every fifth guest spent at the reception desk of a hotel, and then asking the guest to report on the degree of intimacy in the encounter and to complete the SERVQUAL questionnaire. (To account for potential differences associated with time of the day, front desk Time was assessed for three different periods of the day.)

It might be predicted that Time and Intimacy would not show a simple relationship to the SERVQUAL dimensions. For example, does longer Time or shorter Time yield impressions of Reliability? Obviously, it depends—primarily on what amount of time is satisfactory and/or typical. To account for this, Soteriou and Chase (1998) measured Time and Intimacy as deviations from satisfactory or typical levels of Time and Intimacy. Results revealed a nonlinear relationship between Time and service quality as well as between Intimacy and service quality. This means that, as either Time or Intimacy deviated from what was deemed satisfactory *in either direction,* service quality suffered. In the language of Parasuraman, Berry, and Zeithaml (1991), there was a "zone of tolerance" for Time and Intimacy, such that deviations from this zone resulted in poor service quality experiences. In terms of Time, service quality improves with Time, but only up to a certain amount. Then, there is a zone of tolerance where service quality remains flat as Time increases. If Time increases further, service quality suffers. What is especially useful about this line of research is (a) the documentation of customer contact as multifaceted and (b) the finding that customer-contact dimensions, both Time and Intimacy, can be reliably coded and related to known dimensions of service quality experiences. This should greatly facilitate the inclusion of customer contact into optimization and other OM models.

Revenue Management

Prior to leaving the OM approach to issues of service delivery processes and revenues, we want to introduce the additional concept of revenue (yield) management. Revenue management is based on the idea that resources should be maximally used in the creation of revenues. This idea is intended to apply to all industries, but is especially true for service firms that have resources that cannot be inventoried. Revenue management is all about pricing the service in ways that segment the market such that the total consequences maximizes the potential revenue. Perhaps the best example of the application of revenue-management principles concerns airline travel, where the passengers on any given flight might be traveling at widely different fares. Thus, given that the operating costs for an airline flight are pretty much fixed regardless of the number of passengers on board, it is sensible to have more passengers at any fare for a given flight. Actually it is not the specific *flight* that is critical; it is the entire fleet of flights for an airline that is critical, so revenue-management models do not so much apply to a single flight as they apply to an entire fleet of flights. When there is limited capacity, resources that cannot be inventoried, and the costs associated with providing services are fixed, how should service firms price their services to maximize revenues? Obviously these models have been applied to other service delivery operations: For example, on hotels see Hensdill (1998), and for restaurants see Kelly, Kiefer, and Burdett (1994).

Obviously, revenue-management models focus strongly on revenues—and therefore on the prices that customers pay to generate the revenues. The challenge addressed by revenue-management models is to choose prices that allow the greatest overall profits to be achieved for the firm, balancing the revenues from providing a service with the costs of providing it. In other words, these models provide another way of looking at the operational side of service delivery, considering the costs associated with certain processes as well as the revenue generated by them. It is this consideration of the *costs* of the service that differentiates the concept of revenue management from other related indices of effectiveness, such as *load factor* (i.e., the percentage of an airline flight that has been filled) or *occupancy rate* (i.e., the percentage of hotel rooms filled) (Lovelock, 2001). Obviously, one can fill seats and rooms but lose money in the process. What revenue-management models permit is the opportunity to *optimize* load and occupancy such that the net revenue is maximized.

The statistical models for performing yield management calculations are well known (Simon, 1989), but they are not as straightforward as they might seem at first. On the surface, one determines the pricing pattern that maximizes revenues for a particular airline flight or hotel room or movie theater seat. However, the problem becomes much more complex when other variables are introduced into the mix. For example, an airline that employs the hub-and-spoke system confronts the issue of how to modify the pattern that optimizes revenues per flight in order to optimize revenues for the entire system. That is, because flights are now seen as serving two purposes, getting passengers from A to B and also getting passengers from A to B to take a flight to C, the optimization models become quite complex. Another example might be hotel rooms: People stay varying lengths of time in rooms such that day-to-day calculations depend on considerations of length of stay per room as well as new arrivals (Kimes & Chase, 1998). Despite these complicating factors, however, yield management has successfully been applied in helping service facilities to set prices appropriately in an effort to balance capacity with demand. (For an excellent review of the waiting time literature, see Durrand-Moreau, 1999.)

Conclusion

In this chapter, we have provided a brief introduction to how the field of OM has been brought to bear on issues of service and service quality. It should be clear that there are many things going on in organizations that have an influence over customer experiences that are not considered by marketing or HRM/OB perspectives. Namely, OM scholars have provided some keen insights into the consequences of having customers participate in the processes of service delivery, and have been working on operationalizing this idea of customer contact to facilitate further research in the area. The chapter also highlights another contribution of OM to services: its emphasis on costs, returns, *net* profits, and so forth. In this regard, OM brings marketing and OB/HRM into the world of dollars and cents, where most firms operate. It makes little sense to recommend clever and innovative processes for delivering service quality—even if they will yield immensely satisfied customers—without a consideration of the costs associated with the processes.

As we have mentioned before, the work done in the field of OM has held little interest to scholars in other realms—particularly those of the OB persuasion. Given the importance of the issues addressed by OM, we might be well served to ask, how the operational and behavioral worlds can be drawn together. For example, consider the recent discussion of revenue management: We might ask, how do decisions about filling airplane seats or hotel rooms have consequences for the people who work in planes and hotels? Are there optimal levels for the creation and maintenance of a service climate that, while not optimizing revenues in the short term, do so in the long term because of word-of-mouth advertising by customers or job satisfaction of employees, which produces superior job applicants due to reputation as a superior place to work?

From an immediate revenue standpoint, the issue is clear: Since the plane will fly that flight on that day only once, then calculate the net revenue benefits of filling it up; if the room will only exist once on that day in the hotel, then calculate the net revenue benefits of putting someone in the bed. But, what about the staffing concerns of a fuller flight? Do fuller flights require more training of cabin attendants? Do fuller hotels require superior reward-and-recognition systems for motivating hotel staff? A full plane may require more staff than a less full plane and those who staff such full flights may require additional training in the way of crowd control and, especially, assisting passengers in the case of emergencies. Fuller flights also create "emotion work" (Hochschild, 1983) issues. Emotion work refers to jobs in which people must always be "on" because they are in constant public contact. The larger the crowd and the more intense the relationship becomes, the more emotional control is required by such workers. Fuller flights require more work, not only in the service acts we typically consider (e.g., serving passengers meals, finding blankets and pillows), but in doing all of this with a smile. We do not wish to belabor this issue, but simply to point out the potential for various research perspectives on service quality to mingle together to address issues. The interplay of OM decisions, marketing decisions, and OB/HRM decisions will be a useful focus later in the book

For now, we conclude with the thought that the presence of the customer in the organization and the participation of the customer in production of his or her own service, as well as the interactions of such customers with employees, have received surprisingly little attention from HRM/OB researchers. In the next chapter, we turn to the service topics on which HRM/OB researchers have been focusing.

Notes

1. Furthermore, McLaughlin (1996) goes so far as to say not only that variability can never be fully eliminated, but that sometimes it should not even be of central concern. He notes that the penchant for reducing variability overlooks the fact that reducing the *mean* may be a more important goal. For example, waiting time is a strong cause of customer dissatisfaction, so finding ways to reduce that mean can be useful—even if variability around the mean remains at the same level. In fact, research shows that reductions in the mean waiting time have significant effects on customer satisfaction and that no other manipulations (e.g., different forms of queues, distractions while waiting) had much of an effect on satisfaction (Durrand-Moreau, 1999). Thus, at least in the waiting-line literature, the average, and not manipulations of variability, seems to matter the most.

2. Another noteworthy feature of the Bitner et al. (1997) work is its summary of the chronology of research on customer participation in production (see their Table II, p. 196). Also see Rodie and Kleine (2000) for a review of the literature on customer participation in production.

3. In actuality, service quality data were collected separately for an examination area and a financial screening area, and the linkage analyses were also run separately. Only occasional differences in results were found for the examination area and the financial screening area.

4. The annual revenue impact is calculated by taking the differential ($2.80) and multiplying it by the number of rooms (on average, 200 rooms) to determine the impact per day. This number ($560) is then multiplied by 365 to arrive at the annual impact.

5. The Communication Time, Information Richness, and Intimacy data were generated using scaling procedures that revealed excellent reliability across observers. This means that when two or more people observed an episode and rated it for these three variables, they tended to agree on their ratings.

References

Bateson, J. E. G. (1983). The self-service customer—empirical findings. In L. Berry, G. L. Shostack, & G. D. Upah (Eds.), *Emerging perspectives in services marketing* (pp. 50–53). Chicago: American Marketing Association.

Bitner, M. J., Faranda, W. T., Hubbert, A. R., & Zeithaml, V. (1997). Customer contributions and roles in service delivery. *International Journal of Service Industry Management, 8,* 193–205.

Cermak, D. S. P., File, K. M., & Prince, R. A. (1994). A benefit segmentation of the major donor market. *Journal of Business Research, 29*(2), 121–130.

Chase, R. B. (1978). Where does the customer fit in a service operation? *Harvard Business Review, 56,* 137–142.

Chase, R. B. (1981). The customer contact approach to services: Theoretical bases and practical extensions. *Operations Research, 4,* 698–706.

Chase, R. B., & Aquilano, N. J. (1977). *Production and operations management: A life-cycle approach.* Homewood, IL: Irwin.

Chase, R. B., Northcraft, G. B., & Wolf, G. (1984). Designing high contact service systems: Application to branches of a savings and loan. *Decision Sciences, 15,* 542–556.

Chase, R. B., & Stewart, D. M. (1994). Make your service fail-safe. *Sloan Management Review, 35,* 35–45.

Chase, R. B., & Tansik, D. A. (1983). The customer contact model for organizational design. *Management Science, 29,* 1037–1050.

Cronin, J. J., Jr., & Taylor, T. S. (1992). Measuring service quality: A reexamination and extension. *Journal of Marketing, 56,* 55–69.

Cronin, J. J., Jr., & Taylor, T. S. (1994). SERVPERF versus SERVQUAL: Reconciling performance-based and perceptions-minus-expectations measurement of service quality. *Journal of Marketing, 58,* 125–131.

Do-it yourself grocery check-out. (1994, January). *The Wall Street Journal,* p. B1.

Dorsch, J. J., Yasin, M. M., & Czuchry, A. J. (1997). Application of root cause analysis in a service delivery operation environment: A framework for implementation. *International Journal of Service Industry Management, 8,* 268–289.

Durrand-Moreau, A. (1999). Waiting for service: Ten years of empirical research. *International Journal of Service Industry Management, 10,* 171–189.

Fitzimmons, J. A., & Fitzimmons, M. J. (1994). *Service management for competitive advantage.* New York: McGraw-Hill.

Garvin, D. A. (1988). *Managing quality: The strategic and competitive edge.* New York: Free Press.

Hensdill, C. (1998, March). The culture of revenue management. *Hotels,* pp. 83–86.

Hochschild, A. R. (1983). *The managed heart: Commercialization of human feeling.* Berkeley: University of California Press.

Kellogg, D. L., & Chase, R. B. (1995). Constructing an empirically derived measure for customer contact. *Management Science, 41,* 1734–1749.

Kelly, T. J., Kiefer, N. M., & Burdett, K. (1994). A demand-based approach to menu pricing. *Cornell Hotel and Restaurant Administration Quarterly, 34,* 40–45.

Kimes, S. E. (1999). The relationship between product quality and revenue per available room at Holiday Inn. *Journal of Service Research, 2,* 138–144.

Kimes, S. E., & Chase, R. B. (1998). The strategic levers of yield management. *Journal of Service Research, 1,* 156–166.

Lengnick-Hall, C. A. (1996). Customer contributions to quality: A different view of the customer-oriented firm. *Academy of Management Review, 21,* 791–824.

Lovelock, C. H. (1983). Classifying services to gain strategic marketing insights. *Journal of Marketing, 47,* 9–20.

Lovelock, C. H. (2001). *Services marketing: People, technology, strategy* (4th ed.). Englewood Cliffs, NJ: Prentice Hall.

Lovelock, C. H., & Young, R. F. (1979). Look to consumers to increase productivity. *Harvard Business Review, 57,* 168–178.

McLaughlin, C. (1996). Why variation reduction is not everything: A new paradigm for service operations. *International Journal of Service Industry Management, 7,* 17–30.

Orsingher, C. (1999). *Il servizio dalla parte del cliente: Un approccio cognitivo all'esperienza di consume.* Rome, Italy: Carocci editore.

Parasuraman, A., Berry, L., & Zeithaml, V. (1991). Understanding customer expectations of service. *Sloan Management Review, 32*(3), 39–48.

Rodie, A. R., & Kleine, S. S. (2000). Customer participation in services production and delivery. In T. A. Swartz & D. Iacobucci (Eds.), *Handbook of services marketing and management* (pp. 111–126). Thousand Oaks, CA: Sage.

Rust, R. T., Zahorik, A. J., & Keiningham, T. L. (1995). Return on quality (ROQ): Making service quality financially accountable. *Journal of Marketing, 59,* 58–70.

Salancik, G. R. (1977). Commitment and the control of organizational behavior and belief. In B. M. Staw & G. R. Salancik (Eds.), *New directions in organizational behavior* (pp. 1–54). Chicago: St. Clair.

Schneider, B., & Bowen, D. E. (1995). *Winning the service game.* Boston: Harvard Business School Press.

Simon, H. (1989). *Price management.* New York: North-Holland.

Solomon, C. (1993, August 4). Self-service at gas stations includes paying. *The Wall Street Journal,* p. B1.

Soteriou, A. C., & Chase, R. B. (1998). Linking the customer contact model to service quality. *Journal of Operations Management, 16,* 495–508.

Soteriou, A. C., & Chase, R. B. (in press). A robust optimization approach for improving service quality. *Manufacturing and Service Operations Management.*

Zahorik, A. J., Rust, R. T., & Keiningham, T. L. (2000). Estimating the return on quality: Providing insights into profitable investments in service quality. In T. A. Swartz & D. Iacobucci (Eds.), *Handbook of services marketing and management* (pp. 223–245). Thousand Oaks, CA: Sage.

Zeithaml, V. A., & Bitner, M. J. (2000). *Services marketing: Integrating customer focus across the firm* (2nd ed.). New York: McGraw-Hill.

4 Service Climate

In this chapter, we are going to venture directly into the world of organizational behavior. However, we are not going to take the typical approach of discussing topics like employee motivation and leadership in general. Rather, we will attempt to capture the degree to which members of service firms experience motivational tactics and organizational leadership as focused on delivering superior service quality to customers. For present purposes, we view the importance of these organizational behaviors in terms of how they focus people in organizations on service quality.

Let's briefly review how we got here. In Chapter 1, we presented some history on the thinking about quality in organizations, especially quality as conceptualized in manufacturing firms. We introduced the idea that the differences between services and goods translated into differences in the nature of what quality means for services and goods. In Chapter 2, we took a very close look at service quality, examining its definition and measurement. In that chapter, it began to become clear that service quality was dependent upon customer experiences with a service delivery firm and that the firm itself might therefore require examination for the procedures it used to deliver service. We consequently devoted Chapter 3 to looking at services processes that allow organizations to cope with the variability that customers introduce into the calculus of service quality. In that chapter, the links between the quality of service delivery processes and revenues and profits were particularly salient.

Now, in the present chapter, we are going to stay inside the organization and focus on people issues. We will look at the way the internal life of the organization functions as a strategic entity focused on service quality (Schneider, 2000). So, in contrast to Chapter 3, which focused on service processes themselves, we currently direct our attention to the human, or employee, component of service delivery.

As a way of focusing on the human component of internal organizational functioning, recall the service profit chain described in Chapter 1 (Heskett, Sasser, & Schlesinger, 1997): internal service quality → employee satisfaction → employee loyalty → external service quality. In the following pages, we will discuss issues of organizational design that should enable an organization to set this service profit chain in motion. In particular, we will discuss the internal functioning of the organization in terms of organizational climate—especially the climate for service.[1] Following an introduction to the generic world of organizational climate, we will discuss climate for service and what has been called *linkage research*. This latter section will focus on the research that has linked the internal functioning variable of climate for service to external criteria, such as customer experiences of service quality and customer satisfaction.

Defining Climate

In studying organizational climate, we are essentially studying organizational issues—such as service quality—in terms of what employees in organizations report they experience. This is a decidedly psychological perspective for describing and understanding organizational functioning. A climate approach looks at organizational behavior through the lens of the actors, and the lens makes certain assumptions about how actors process the world around them and how they attach meaning to this world. In contrast, then, to independent examination of the structural properties of firms, or the physical layout of firms, or the frequency with which hotels reveal defects when inspected by trained inspectors, here we view organizations as the perceptions members have of them. In other words, the perspective we take here is that organizations are defined as much by the experiences and perceptions of their members as by their structure, their physical layout, and other seemingly more objective data that may exist on or about them. For us, organizations are clearly defined by what members say they are. Organizational climate is one way to conceptualize the totality of the experiences organizational members have of their work organization. Thus, rather than defining climate in terms of what an organization's CEO says that it should be or what a recruiting brochure says that it is, our definition of climate rests on what employees actually report experiencing in their organization.

Employees tend to form their perceptions by considering (a) how the daily business of the organization is conducted and (b) what goals the organization appears to be pursuing (Schneider, Brief, & Guzzo 1996). The organization transmits this information to employees through the policies, practices, and procedures that it has in place (e.g., human resources policies, marketing practices, operations management procedures). These practices, policies, and procedures collectively send messages about what is important—what behaviors the organization rewards, supports, and expects. Based on the behaviors and activities for which they receive rewards and support, employees develop a summary sense of the answer to the question "What is important around here?" This answer represents organizational climate.

In other words, climate represents the *patterns* or *themes* that employees perceive in what they experience; it is the sense they make from the individual experiences they have (Weick, 1995). Thus it is not any one human resource policy or any one training program or any one advertising campaign that determines climate: Climate is all about the perception of the theme that might tie these together to create meaning beyond the specific elements of experience.

Although the construct of climate has been in the organizational psychological literature in some form or another for more than 60 years, it is still surrounded by controversy. For example, a great deal of attention has been paid to debating how climate and culture are the same as or different (Schneider, 2000). The climate construct has also had to survive attacks that it was the same thing as job satisfaction (Guion, 1973), although this issue was largely put to rest by demonstrating that climate and job satisfaction are often only weakly correlated with each other (LaFollette & Sims, 1975; Schneider & Snyder, 1975). Perhaps the major controversies surrounding the construct concerned (a) the inconsistency of results surrounding the relationship between climate and such organizational outcomes as sales or productivity and (b) the appropriate level of analysis at which climate should be conceptualized and studied.

With regard to the first issue, our perspective is that inconsistency in the relationship between climate reports and organizational outcomes is largely due to a failure to conceptually link the *kind* of climate conceptualized and assessed to the outcome of interest. The fact is that there have been many conceptualizations and measures of climate, and these varieties of measures have been related to almost every conceivable organizational outcome—with the result being inconsistency in relationships between such measures and such outcomes (Schneider, 1975). For example, consider McGregor's (1960) conceptualization of managerial climate as a climate of trust. What would be the expected relationship between employee reports that they worked in a climate of trust and customer satisfaction? While it is possible to come up with some rationalization for such a relationship, we propose that the likelihood is stronger that a climate for service would demonstrate a relationship with customer satisfaction.

The second issue, the level-of-analysis issue, has also been one that has received considerable attention. We deal with it now, because the level-of-analysis issue is also central to the inconsistency in relationships found between measures of organizational climate and important organizational outcomes.

Levels-of-Analysis Issues

Previously, we discussed organizational climate as employees' experiences of what is important in their organization—what policies, practices, and procedures focus on and what gets rewarded, supported, and expected. A critical element of this perspective is that it rests on what *employees experience*, not what is written down in some policy manual, merit reward–system document, or mission statement. In defining climate in terms of employee experiences, it is important to note that experiences are those of individual employees. Given the nature of perceptions, we must address our reasoning for discussing the construct of *organizational* climate based (typically) on the survey responses of *individuals*.

In the realm of climate research, the level-of-analysis debate has centered on whether climate should be defined at the individual or group (i.e., organization) level. In other words, should the individual perceptions of employees be combined to form the construct of organizational climate, or should the construct be left at the individual level? Those who advocate measuring climate at an individual level maintain that people perceive their environments in subjective ways and that it is conceptually difficult to combine idiosyncratic perceptions together to create an organizational climate index (James, James, & Ashe, 1990). If one employee described his or her organization's climate as a 10 in terms of being nonparticipative, and another employee described it as a 0, would it make sense to describe the climate as moderately participative with a rating of 5? This would not describe the climate that either employee was experiencing, and the disagreement calls into question the appropriateness of averaging the scores together.

However, in an alternative scenario, suppose the employees both rated the climate as a 5. In this case, averaging the employees' ratings together to form an organizational climate score of 5 would perfectly describe the perceived environment for both employees. More importantly, similar ratings from different employees indicate that they are experiencing the environment in the same way. To the extent that employees agree in their perceptions of the environment, it makes sense to represent this sharedness by defining climate as a group-level construct. In terminology that is still used today, James and Jones (1974) described individuals' perceptions of their environments as *psychological climates* and the combination of these individuals' perceptions at the group or organizational level as *organizational climate*.

Thus we have argued that it makes sense to combine the perceptions of individuals into a group-level construct—when those individuals agree and when the outcome of interest is a group-level construct.[2] We are agreeing to define climate as the combination of individual perceptions of climate only when these individual perceptions reveal specified levels of agreement and/or interrater reliability. The next question that arises is whether agreement should be expected among employees within an organization. The answer of proponents of the construct of organizational climate is yes.

Climate may in a real sense be a subjective world, but the evidence is now clear that there is sharedness among people as to what that subjective world is like (Schneider, Bowen, Ehrhart, & Holcombe, 2000). As James et al. (1990) note, there are a number of forces acting on employees to create similarity in perceptions. For example, as described by Schneider's attraction-selection-attrition model, people within organizations tend to be similar to each other on many dimensions, so they may very well share similar experiences there (Schneider, 1987). There is therefore a strong possibility that they will report their perceptions of their environments in similar ways. Furthermore, social influences from other members in the organization might result in individuals interpreting their environment in similar ways. People are always talking about this and that in organizations, discussing their boss or upper-level management policies or the state of the equipment and resources they have to work with, and so forth. These conversations can yield shared images of the organization and come to be the reality of the organization for those who participate in such discussions (see Martin, 1992, 2002; Schein, 1992; Schneider & Reichers, 1983; Trice & Beyer, 1993). Given that agreement among employees is a central aspect of our definition of organizational climate, we will now turn our attention to assessing agreement in climate perceptions. That is, it is one thing to assume there is agreement and it is another thing to document that sufficient agreement exists for aggregation.

Measurement Considerations as Levels-of-Analysis Issues. The idea of deriving the meaning of organizational climate from the aggregation of individual responses gained a great deal of acceptance from the introduction of aggregation statistics into the climate literature (Jones & James, 1979; Roberts, Hulin, & Rousseau, 1978; Rousseau, 1985; Schneider, 1985). These aggregation statistics provided researchers an objective, quantifiable method of determining how much agreement existed within a group, and they also gave some broad guidelines for how much agreement is enough in terms of trying to justify aggregating a construct to the group level. Statistics, such as r_{wg}, WABA, ICC(1), and ICC(2), can all be used to determine whether agreement exists—an issue that directly bears on the meaning of the climate construct. These statistics are briefly described in Box 4.1 and are summarized nicely in Bliese (2000).

Box 4.1   Description of Aggregation Techniques Used in Climate
            Research

$$r_{wg}$$

The most popular measure of within-group agreement is probably r_{wg} (see, for example, James, Demaree, & Wolf, 1984). Essentially, r_{wg} compares the variance that exists among ratings within a group to an expected distribution of ratings. A higher r_{wg} indicates a closer absolute match between the actual distribution of ratings and the expected one, with an r_{wg} of 1.00 indicating that the actual and the expected distribution of ratings were the same. With the uniform distribution typically used in climate research, this would imply that all of the ratings were the same number and would justify the aggregation of the individual ratings to the group level. (It is important to note that r_{wg} is a measure of absolute agreement. If one person's pattern of responses were 2, 2, 3, 3, 4, and another person's were 3, 3, 4, 4, 5, then r_{wg} would be zero—indicating no agreement.) Given that perfect agreement and zero agreement are unlikely in practice, the question arises of how

Box 4.1   Continued

much agreement is enough to justify aggregation. There is no definitive answer to this question, but a general rule is that r_{wg} should be at least 0.60 (James, 1982).

WABA

Another technique used in determining if data may be aggregated to the group level is known as WABA, standing for Within-And-Between Analysis (see, for example, Dansereau & Alutto, 1990). In WABA, individual responses from multiple groups on two variables, X and Y, are correlated. This total correlation is broken into "within" and "between" components. The within component represents the proportion of the variance in the total correlation due to variance *within* the groups being analyzed, while the between component represents the variance *between* the different groups. According to WABA logic, aggregation is justified when people in a group agree more with one another than they do with people in other groups. For more detail, see Yammarino and Markham (1992) and George and James (1993).

ICC(1) and ICC(2)

Intraclass correlations (ICCs) are also frequently encountered in analyses of group-level constructs. The two most prominent ICCs are ICC(1) and ICC(2). ICCs assess reliability; by this, we mean that absolute agreement (as in r_{wg}) is not required. What is required is that the pattern of responses be similar. ICC(1) is a comparison of the variance that exists among ratings within groups to the variance that exists in ratings between groups. In conceptual terms, ICC(1) is an indication of how much of the variance in individual ratings can be explained by group membership. To justify aggregation, it is desirable to be able to attribute as much variance as possible to the group level, so that high ICC(1)s can be taken as support for aggregation. While there is no set level of how high an ICC(1) should be, James (1982) reported a median ICC(1) of 0.12 in the organizational literature.

(Continued)

Box 4.1   Continued

ICC(2) also examines between-group variance relative to within-group variance (Bartko, 1976). However, ICC(2) is a measure of group-mean reliability. That is, it indicates if groups can be reliability-differentiated from each other by their means. As a rule of thumb, Glick (1985) recommends an ICC(2) cutoff of 0.60 in doing group-level analyses. Note that ICC(2) statistics are perfectly correlated with the one-way ANOVA when applied to group means.

Using Aggregation Statistics

In comparing the techniques for justifying aggregation, it is important to note that only r_{wg} is a measure of within-group agreement. This is the only one of the measures that is designed to reflect the level of absolute consensus that exists within a group. Thus, technically, demonstrating an adequate r_{wg} value should be sufficient for justifying the aggregation of individual, psychological climate responses to form an organizational climate score. However, what the r_{wg} does not show is whether there are group-level effects. WABA and ICCs are designed to answer this question. That is, WABA and ICCs ask the question of whether there is sufficient variance at the group level of analysis to allow the group-level construct to relate to other group-level constructs.

Demonstrating that groups differ from each other is not necessary for demonstrating that people within a group agree (see, for example, George & James, 1993). Under the direct consensus composition model that we have used to define organizational climate, we specified only that people within a group must agree—not that groups must differ from each other. However, without between-group differences, relationships at the group level of analysis cannot exist. In other words, if all groups score identically on variable A, there will be no variance for this variable at the group level, and therefore across groups variable A cannot be correlated with any other attribute on which the groups might differ. In effect, then, from the standpoint of relationships among variables, a lack of group-level variability calls into question the meaningfulness of a group-level construct.

Box 4.1   Continued

In a sense, the level at which variability exists in a data set might be taken as an indication of the level to which data should be aggregated. Thus, if no between-team variability exists but there is variability at the organization level, perhaps data should be aggregated to the higher level of organization instead of the lower level of team. This perspective is still being debated in the multilevel research literature (Chan, 1998). For a complete discussion of conceptual and statistical issues regarding level of analysis issues, see Klein and Kozlowski (2000).

Focused Climates

In introducing the concept of organizational climate, we defined it as employees' perceptions of the *environment* in which they worked. We then added the specification that individual perceptions must agree to define climate at the unit (group, organizational) level. We will now turn our attention to what we meant by the term *environment*.

In early organizational climate research, *climate* typically referred to almost everything that happened to and around employees. A climate survey might ask employees for their perceptions of several different aspects of their working environment, including their leader, the reward system under which they work, the kind of training they received to do their job, and so forth. While these types of surveys were useful for gathering data on general employee viewpoints, Schneider (1975) concluded that these measures were too broad and inclusive to be easily understood or interpreted, and too generic to be of use for any specific outcome or outcomes of interest. In their efforts to capture all aspects of the environment in their items, the surveys developed were too unfocused and amorphous either to provide actionable information to organizations or to statistically link to specific outcomes of interest. As Schneider et al. (2000) point out, it is difficult to determine what general construct is being measured by a 10-dimension survey of generic organizational climate dimensions.

To help climate research gain focus, Schneider (1975) proposed that climate surveys should not attempt to measure generic organizational climate, but rather that they should try to measure an organization's climate *for something*. In other words, he suggested that climate measures should have a specific focus—which might be as diverse as a climate for safety (Zohar, 2000), a climate for sexual harassment (Fitzgerald, Drasgow, Hulin, Gelfand, & Magley, 1997), a climate for employee well-being (Burke, Borucki, & Hurley, 1992), or (of particular interest to the current chapter) a climate for service. Thus, while a general climate measure might ask employees about leadership, rewards, and training, a climate-for-service measure would focus on the leadership behaviors related to service (e.g., planning for service, setting goals for service), rewards and recognition for delivering excellent service, and the degree to which service quality is emphasized in training programs.[3]

Climate for Service

The type of climate most relevant to the study of service quality is a climate for service. Drawing on our previous discussions of the climate construct, we define *service climate* as the shared employee perceptions of the policies, practices, and procedures and the behaviors that get rewarded, supported, and expected with regard to customer service and customer service quality. Basically, a service climate represents the degree to which the internal functioning of an organization is experienced as one focused on service quality. As noted earlier, it is a pattern across policies, procedures, and rewarded behaviors to which employees attach the meaning, "Service quality is important here." So, when employees perceive that they are rewarded for delivering quality service *and* when employees perceive that management devotes time, energy, and resources to service quality *and* when employees receive the training they require to effectively deal with diverse customers, *then* a positive service climate is more likely to be the theme or meaning attached to these experiences.

Given a definition of service climate, the next challenge facing a service climate researcher is measurement. In Chapter 2, we discussed the measurement of service quality from the customer point of view, and we presented several different sets of dimensions that might underlie customer perceptions of service quality (e.g., Reliability, Tangibles, Empathy, Assurance, and Responsiveness). A similar perspective can be taken toward explicating the service climate construct, with the intent of uncovering the dimensions of internal organizational functioning that (a) constitute the elements of the gestalt indicating service climate and

(b) allow and encourage the delivery of quality service. Furthermore, a methodology similar to the one used for determining service quality dimensions has been employed for determining service climate dimensions. Just as the SERVQUAL program began with customer interviews (Parasuraman, Zeithaml, & Berry, 1985), Schneider also began his service climate work with interviews—this time, with employees (Schneider, Parkington, & Buxton, 1980).

One goal we have in this section of the chapter is to parse service climate into manageable elements. The development of service climate measures and the collection of climate-related data can look daunting to people just getting into this research arena. Thus we tackle the issues below to help readers get a handle on actually working with the construct of service climate, rather than simply considering it in the abstract. Hopefully, this will help researchers approaching this domain for the first time.

In a series of early climate studies, Schneider et al. (1980) and Schneider and Bowen (1985) studied employees from branches of two large banks to develop a measure of service climate. The researchers were careful to conduct focus groups with employees representing several different positions in the branches, including managers, tellers, and platform people (those who sit at desks and open and close accounts, issue CDs, and so forth). The employees were asked to respond to general, open-ended questions about their bank branch in order to gain a sense of the kinds of experiences they had at work that told them that service was (or was not) important. The goal of the interview questions was to generate specific service-related policies, practices, procedures and behaviors that employees felt were expected, rewarded, and supported related to service.

An informal content analysis of the issues that emerged from the employee interviews yielded seven dimensions of service climate (Schneider et al., 1980). The dimensions are shown in the left column of Table 4.1. To measure these dimensions of service climate, survey items were created to tap each dimension. Great efforts were made to focus the items in the survey on specific behaviors, because these, in the collective, are what describe the elements of climate. For example, the scale of Managerial Functions was composed of behaviorally oriented items, such as "My branch manager gets the people in different jobs to work together in serving customers" and "My branch manager takes the time to help new employees learn about the branch and its customers."

Table 4.1   Service Climate Dimensions

Schneider et al. (1980) Dimensions	Schneider & Bowen (1985) Dimensions
Managerial Functions Bank branch manager's efforts to plan, coordinate, set goals, and establish routines for giving good service	*Branch Management* Relabeling of Managerial Functions scale
Effort Rewarded Extent to which extra effort in serving customers was rewarded/appreciated	*No clear loading*
Retain Customers Extent to which there were active attempts to retain customers in the bank branch	*Customer Attention/Retention* Relabeling of Retain Customers scale
Personnel Support Extent to which employees felt that other personnel supported them in their efforts to deliver service *Central Processing Support* Extent to employees felt that the bank's processing of records and paperwork supported them in their efforts to deliver service *Marketing Support* Extent to which employees felt that the marketing department supported them in their efforts to deliver service	*Systems Support* Personnel, Central Processing, and Marketing Support were collapsed into one Systems Support scale
Equipment/Supply Support Extent to which employees felt that the equipment and supplies were sufficient and reliable enough to support them in their efforts to deliver service	*Logistics Support* Relabeling of Equipment/Supply Support scale

SOURCE: Based on Schneider et al. (1980) and Schneider and Bowen (1985).

For the original Schneider et al. (1980) publication, the seven dimensions of service climate that emerged from the content analysis were retained for analysis. Later, Schneider and Bowen (1985) submitted the original data to a principal components factor analysis with orthogonal rotation.[4] This analysis yielded a set of four dimensions that collectively defined service climate. The dimensions found by Schneider and Bowen (1985) are listed in the right column of Table 4.1.

Recall that Schneider and his colleagues (Schneider et al., 1980; Schneider & Bowen, 1985) conceptualized service climate at the bank branch level. Each branch of the bank was essentially considered its own organization, such that climate was analyzed at the organization level. The service climate responses of the employees within each branch were averaged to form a branch score on each service climate scale, and aggregation was justified in an application of the direct consensus composition model (in which agreement is required for aggregation).[5] However, Schneider and Bowen (1985) made the argument that the branch was the *only* appropriate unit of analysis for this kind of study— regardless of whether employees agreed on their perceptions of the climate for service (an additive composition model). They noted that customers get served by different tellers at different times of the day and on different visits to the branch, so that it is really their impression of the branch as a whole that matters. Furthermore, if it is the experiences of the branch's customers that are the criteria of interest, then it is necessary to aggregate employee perceptions to the branch level of analysis.

The dimensions found by Schneider et al. (1980) and Schneider and Bowen (1985) are certainly not definitive in capturing service climate. As in the efforts to measure service quality, several researchers have developed service climate dimensions that are different from those shown in Table 4.1. For example, in a later study, Schneider, White, and Paul (1998) worked with a three-factor model of service climate. These three factors are presented in Table 4.2.

There has been little effort in the service climate literature to develop a universal set of service climate dimensions, and the question of whether such a set exists has received much less attention in the service climate literature than the parallel question has received in the service quality literature. Thus, unlike the development of SERVQUAL, one service climate measure has yet to dominate service climate research. However, in 1998, Lytle, Hom, and Mokwa did develop a service climate survey they labeled as SERV*OR (i.e., Service Orientation). Their methodology was similar to that used by Schneider et al. (1980) in the development of their service climate survey, but, like the development of SERVQUAL, SERV*OR was based on studying organizations from multiple industries. The authors employed focus group interviews, pretesting of items, multisample assessment of the items (e.g., factor analyses of the items), and multi-industry replication of their survey. The 10 dimensions of service climate that they identified are presented in Table 4.3.

The conceptualizations of service climate that we have presented above (e.g., Lytle et al., 1998; Schneider & Bowen, 1985; Schneider

Table 4.2   Service Climate Dimensions and Sample Items Like Those Used in
                Schneider et al. (1998)

Customer Orientation
Measures the degree to which an organization emphasizes, in multiple ways, meeting
customer needs and expectations for service quality
  Sample item:
  • "We keep customers informed of changes which affect them."

Managerial Practices
Reflects those actions taken by an employee's immediate manager that support and
reward the delivery of quality service
  Sample item:
  • "My manager supports our focus on the importance of service quality."

Customer Feedback
Assesses the practice of soliciting *and using* feedback from customers regarding ser-
vice quality
  Sample item:
  • "We get feedback about how our external customers evaluate the quality of
    service we deliver."

---

et al., 1980; Schneider et al., 1998) give an idea of the kinds of issues
that might be covered in a service climate survey. For example, a common theme running through all of the measures is a focus on the treatment of external customers and on basic managerial practices with
respect to service. Furthermore, items referring to listening to customers appeared in both the Schneider et al. (1998) and Lytle et al.
(1998) representations of climate; this might therefore be another
dimension to include in a service climate survey. Like the service quality measures, the exact dimensions to be included will likely depend on
issues that are of concern in particular organizations or industries.

In using a set of dimensions to measure service climate, the same problems that were faced in the service quality literature present themselves.
Namely, we are measuring a series of climate dimensions to capture a
phenomenon that is essentially a gestalt—the overall service climate. Just
as we presented the point that service quality is an overall judgment
about the service received, we note here that the climate construct (even
when focused on a particular topic, such as service quality) is a gestalt.
That is, service climate represents a summary or overall sense of an
organization's service orientation. Thus, just as service quality measures

Table 4.3   Service Climate Dimensions and Sample Items Adapted From
SERV*OR (Lytle et al., 1998, pp. 484–486)

Servant Leadership
Extent to which leaders of organization display service-oriented behaviors to their
employees—leading by example with regards to service
    Sample item: "Managers give personal input and leadership into creating quality service."

Service Vision
Extent to which leaders have and espouse a vision for being a service-oriented
organization
    Sample item: "There is a true commitment to service, not just lip service."

Customer Treatment
Degree to which organization treats customers in ways that will enhance customer
satisfaction
    Sample item: "Employees go the 'extra mile' for customers."

Employee Empowerment
Degree to which employees have responsibility and authority to meet customer needs
    Sample item: "Employees have freedom and authority to act independently in order
    to provide excellent service."

Service Training
Training in teamwork, problem solving, interpersonal skills, etc., that contribute to the
delivery of quality service
    Sample item: "Every employee receives personal skills training that enhances his/her
    ability to deliver high-quality service."

Service Rewards
Extent to which employees are recognized, rewarded, and compensated to deliver
quality service
    Sample item: "Management provides excellent incentives and rewards at all levels
    for service quality, not just productivity."

Service Failure Prevention
Practices that proactively prevent service failures
    Sample item: "We go out of our way to prevent customer problems."

Service Failure Recovery
Practices that function to respond effectively to customer complaints or service failures
    Sample item: "We provide follow-up service calls to confirm that our services are
    being provided properly."

Service Technology
Organization's use of technology and technology-based systems to serve customers
    Sample item: "We enhance our service capabilities through the use of 'state of the
    art' technology."

(Continued)

Table 4.3 (Continued)

Service Standards Communication
Extent to which service standards or benchmarks are understood by employees throughout the organization
Sample item: Every effort is made to explain the results of customer research to every employee in understandable terms.

SOURCE: Copyright © 1998 by New York University Press. Used by permission.

should include an overall scale to tap service quality directly, service climate researchers might consider including an overall climate scale to directly assess employees' perceptions of the strength of their organization's service climate. For example, a researcher might ask respondents to rate items such as *My organization cares about delivering quality service* and *I am expected to emphasize service quality in my daily work.*

As a middle ground between asking for overall perceptions of climate and assessing individual facets, Schneider et al. (1998) included a scale that they labeled *Global Service Climate* in their study. Each of the items they included was designed to represent a separable facet of the more global service climate construct such that the aggregate across all of the items represented the more global gestalt of service climate. Items like those used to define this service climate gestalt are shown in Table 4.4.

When employees are asked to respond to items assessing these attributes of their work setting, the measure reveals good internal consistency reliability, good interrater agreement within units, and significant relationships with independent ratings of service quality and customer

Table 4.4   Global Service Climate Items Like Those Used in Schneider et al. (1998)

---

1. Rate the job knowledge and skills of your fellow employees to deliver excellent quality service.
2. Rate efforts made by your company to assess the quality of the service it provides.
3. Rate the praise and rewards you and your fellow employees get when you deliver excellent service.
4. Rate the leadership shown by management in your company to enhance service quality.
5. Rate how effectively your company communicates with both employees and customers.
6. Rate the climate for service in your business.

SOURCE: Copyright © 2003 by Personnel Research Associates, Inc. Used by permission. Not to be duplicated or used without explicit written permission.

satisfaction by customers. This connection or linkage of service climate to customer experiences is a topic we will explore below in considerable detail.

For now, it is worth commenting on the fact that the development of measures of both customer experiences of service quality and employee experiences of service climate has followed similar paths. Controversies over definitions have plagued both areas of study, yielding debate over the dimensions of each construct. Of course, there are debates of a conceptual nature, too, centering on the role of expectations in the service quality debate and the appropriate level of analysis and the appropriate focus of the climate construct in the climate debate. In addition, both literatures have adopted the viewpoint of using direct perceptions in the measurement of the constructs, with service quality typically being measured with customer perceptions and service climate typically being measured with employee perceptions.

It is also interesting to note that the different sets of service climate dimensions that we discussed above were all developed in ways similar to SERVQUAL and other service quality measures. All of the procedures began with interviews of the relevant constituents, followed by identifying preliminary themes in the interview data, developing survey items to tap the identified themes, administering the surveys to relevant respondents, and finally using factor analytic techniques to refine the dimensions tapped by the survey.

We hinted above that there might be a connection between these two kinds of measures—service climate on the one hand and service quality on the other. That is, when we discussed the fact that the overall service climate measure developed by Schneider et al. (1998) *works well,* we noted that data collected with that measure from employees correlated with customer satisfaction. In the next section, we review this idea under the rubric of *linkage research.*

Linkage Research

We have spent a great deal of time on the topic of organizational climate in general and service climate in particular. In this section on linkage research, we provide a major reason for why it is important to study service climate. Specifically, this section is devoted to research that has linked measures of service climate to external criterion measures, such as customer perceptions of service quality and customer satisfaction. In other words, the internal functioning of an organization with respect to service has often been found to be reflected in customers' perceptions of the quality of service they receive and their levels of satisfaction. Additional research shows that these, in turn, are ultimately linked to the profitability of organizations (recall the service profit chain from Chapter 1; Heskett et al., 1997). Thus, through the mediators of service quality and customer satisfaction, a positive climate for service can have beneficial financial impacts on an organization—highlighting its importance as a topic of study.

Early Linkage Studies

In the early 1980s, Schneider and his colleagues began a research program linking employee perceptions about what goes on inside an organization to customer perceptions about their experiences with the organization. Schneider et al. (1980) began their research by using a technique we have recommended several times before—talking directly to the actor. Specifically, Schneider et al. (1980) held interviews with bank branch customers to determine what they considered in determining if the bank had a "warm and friendly" atmosphere. What they found was that customers mentioned many facets of organizational functioning beside such issues as the courtesy of the staff. They mentioned the orderliness of the bank, the state of the equipment and machinery the bank was using, the rate at which tellers turned over in their jobs, and so forth. Thus organizational process issues—in addition to the direct treatment of customers—seemed to influence the way customers viewed the bank branches. Since customers seemed to notice these kinds of organizational phenomena, Schneider and his colleagues reasoned that the experiences employees have with these same phenomena would likely be related to customer perceptions about the service they received. In other words, they hypothesized that service climate would be related to customer perceptions of service quality.

Using service climate scores and customer perception scores aggregated to the bank branch level, Schneider et al. (1980) found support for their hypothesis. They demonstrated a strong and significant relationship across 23 bank branches between employee reports on branch service–related practices, policies, and procedures and customer reports of the quality of the service they received. Thus, at the organization (branch) level, more positive service climates were related to more positive perceptions of service quality. For example, referring to the service climate dimensions reported in Table 4.1, customer perceptions of overall service quality correlated 0.54 ($p < 0.01$) with the scale labeled Managerial Functions and 0.63 ($p < 0.01$) with the Retain Customers scale. Customer perceptions of overall service quality also correlated significantly with Personnel Support and Equipment/Supply Support.

Later Linkage Research

The linkage research begun by Schneider et al. (1980) has continued through to the present. For example, as reported earlier, Schneider and Bowen (1985) replicated the relationships found by Schneider et al. (1980). Furthermore, Schneider et al. (1998) used a different service climate measure and a different customer measure than the previous Schneider studies (Schneider, Ashworth, Higgs, & Carr, 1996; Schneider & Bowen, 1985; Schneider et al., 1980) and still found significant relationships between bank employee perceptions of service climate and bank customers' perceptions about the service they received. Other studies that have found similar results include those by Johnson (1996), Wiley (1991), Schmit and Allscheid (1995), and Hartline and Ferrell (1993). These studies provide further support for the hypothesis that employee experiences are reflected in customer experiences. Accordingly, Heskett et al. (1997) labeled the connection between employee and customer experiences the "satisfaction mirror." These authors described a series of studies that demonstrate this relationship in companies such as MCI, Merry Maids, and Xerox; we will return to the Heskett et al. (1997) research again in Chapter 5.

The studies discussed above leave little doubt that customers' perceptions about organizations are tied to the way that employees perceive their organizations. To provide somewhat more detail about this relationship, we will report on two studies that we have conducted recently. The first (Schneider, White, & Paul, 1997) examines the question of which aspects of service climate are most strongly linked to customer perceptions, and the second (Schneider et al., 1998) examines the issue of causality in the employee-customer relationship.

Relationship Marketing. Recall our discussion of relationship marketing from Chapter 2. We described this trend in marketing theory as organizational attempts to form more long-term relationships with customers, in contrast to one-time, transactional exchanges. The logic of the relationship marketing perspective is that a focus on relationships will generate customer loyalty and commitment—and eventually profits (White & Schneider, 2000). Combining this logic with the linkage research, Schneider et al. (1997) asked whether aspects of service climate that reflected this relationship-marketing perspective would relate more strongly to customer perceptions of service quality than would aspects of service climate related to transactional exchanges.

Using archival data from previous studies, Schneider et al. (1997) demonstrated that relationship-oriented facets of climate and culture were more strongly correlated with customer perceptions of service quality than were transaction or efficiency-oriented facets. Specifically, scales such as Customer Orientation and Enthusiast Orientation were more strongly related to customer perceptions of service quality than were scales such as Systems Support and Bureaucrat Orientation. (See Table 4.1 for scale definitions; Customer Orientation is identified as Customer Attention/Retention in Table 4.1.) It is important to note, though, that the transaction-oriented scales were still significantly related to customer perceptions. Thus, while both relationship- and transaction-oriented aspects of service climate were important, a stronger link existed between customer perceptions and relationship-oriented aspects of service climate. These findings provide support for the perspective that a focus on relationships can affect the way customers perceive an organization, and could potentially affect their behaviors toward it.

Causality. Another recent study conducted by Schneider and his colleagues (Schneider et al., 1998) in the area of linkage research bears on the issue of causality in the employee-customer relationship. The standard perspective in the service quality literature is the one that we have implicitly taken so far: service climate → customer perceptions of service quality (e.g., Burke, Rapinski, Dunlap, & Davison, 1996; Schneider & Bowen, 1993, 1995). In other words, an organization's service climate determines, at least in part, customers' perceptions of the organization. Since services are intangible, customers may compensate for the absence of tangible cues for evaluating service quality by looking to the service-oriented atmosphere of the organization to help evaluate the service they received. Some aspects of service climate will "show" to customers, and may influence their perceptions of service quality.

In support of this perspective, Schneider, Ashworth, et al. (1996) conducted a longitudinal study relating service climate and customer satisfaction. Over an 18-month period, they found a stronger relationship between early service climate measures and later customer satisfaction measures than the reverse. (See Box 4.2 for a description of how the "linkage logic" was used to develop the service climate measure used in the study.) The results showed that service climate measured at the beginning of the time period was reflected more strongly in later customer perceptions than early customer perceptions were in later reports of service climate. These findings provide some support for the idea that employee experiences and perceptions of their work climate vis-à-vis service *cause* customer perceptions.

Box 4.2   Description of Schneider, Ashworth, et al. (1996)
Project

The Schneider, Ashworth, et al. (1996) project deserves some special attention for the way in which it developed its service climate measure. The measure was designed using criterion-keying methodology (Nunnally & Bernstein, 1994). Criterion keying is a technique used in the design of psychometric tests, especially tests of interest and tests that use biographical information for the prediction of performance in organizations. The idea behind criterion keying is that the items scored on the test should only be those that correlate with the criterion of interest. In the present chapter, the criterion of interest is customer satisfaction and the potential predictors are the items on the employee survey.

Schneider, Ashworth, et al. (1996) administered a 39-item survey to the insurance agents in 27 regions of an insurance company. For each of the regions, customer satisfaction data were also collected. The 39 items were then correlated with the customer satisfaction data, and it was found that seven of the survey items (and their subparts) were more strongly correlated with customer satisfaction than were the remainder of the items. The seven items that were strongly correlated with customer satisfaction are shown below.

1. When customer requirements are not met, how often do people in your work group take action so the problem does not occur in the future?

2. How often do you receive feedback as to how satisfied your customers are?

(Continued)

Box 4.2   Continued

3. How much does our company actively solicit input from customers?

4. Would you recommend the purchase of [our company's] insurance to a friend or relative?

5. In the past 12 months, have you had a formal performance appraisal discussion to compare your performance against your goals and performance standards?

6. How much opportunity is there for you to pursue your job and career interests at [our company]?

7. How often does your [immediate manager/team leader] talk to you and your coworkers about how the work of your group contributes to:
   • Customer-focused quality
   • Customer retention
   • Competitive position
   • Customer satisfaction
   • Profitability

First, note that the items that we now know are related to customer satisfaction cover both explicitly service-related issues and some issues related to human resources management. This finding is reminiscent of the Schneider et al. (1998) perspective that service climate requires a foundation in good management (Work Facilitation) as well as a focus on service quality through polices and procedures. A second point to note is that the items presented above would *not* be expected to be useful in any other setting. This set of items was selected because, in this insurance company, these items correlate with customer satisfaction as measured in this insurance company. Thus items developed through criterion keying on a specific sample cannot be expected to generalize to other samples; they cannot be expected to have generalizability beyond the sample on which they were developed. In any one company, the lack of generalizability may be irrelevant, because they are concerned with what happens in their company.

Table 4.5   Relationships Between Employee and Customer Data Over Time

| | Customer Data | | | | | | | |
| | *Quarter 1* | | *Quarter 2* | | *Quarter 3* | | *Quarter 4* | |
	CS	*LR*	*CS*	*LR*	*CS*	*LR*	*CS*	*LR*
Employee Data								
Quarter 1 SCP	0.62	0.52	0.62	0.56	0.63	0.51	0.68	0.55
Quarter 2 SCP	0.47	0.49	0.49	0.45	0.44	0.40	0.51	0.46
Quarter 3 SCP	0.54	0.45	0.46	0.46	0.44	0.28 *(ns)*	0.52	0.43
Quarter 4 SCP	0.44	0.42	0.42	0.38	0.40	0.30 *(ns)*	0.48	0.38

NOTE: $N = 27$ insurance company regions. All correlations are statistically significant at $p < 0.05$ unless marked ns.)

CS = Customer Satisfaction

LR = Likelihood of Renewal

SCP = Service Climate Perception

SOURCE: Adapted from Schneider et al. (1996). Copyright © 1996 by *Personnel Psychology*. Used by permission.

The results of the Schneider, Ashworth, et al. (1996) study are presented above in Table 4.5, with (a) columns of four quarters of data on Customer Satisfaction (CS) and the likelihood of renewing policies in the future (Likelihood of Renewal: LR) and (b) rows of four quarters of employee perceptions of service climate (Service Climate Perceptions: SCP). Note that the SCP first quarter–CS first quarter relationship is 0.62, rising to 0.68 for the SCP first quarter–CS fourth quarter relationship. In general, the employee (SCP) to customer (CS and LR) correlations increased over time, while the customer to employee correlations tended to decrease over time. This suggests that climate causes customer satisfaction rather than the reverse.

While the data in Table 4.5 tend to show stronger relationships going forward from employee data to customer data than the reverse, it is also reasonable to hypothesize that customer perceptions of service quality can cause employee perceptions of service climate. In the purchase of services, there is a great deal of customer-employee interaction when compared to the purchase of goods. It is easy to buy a vacuum cleaner without ever having contact with the organization that produced it, but it is much harder to open a bank account without interacting with bank employees (recall the discussion of the customer-contact model in

Chapter 3). Through this contact, employees may learn about customers' perceptions of the service they receive. Customers in service organizations may communicate to employees instances of good or bad service and how they feel about the quality of the service they have received from the organization. When customers issue reports of good service to employees, this may encourage employees to perceive their service climate in favorable terms. Employees may follow the implicit logic of "It's working, so we must be doing something right." Conversely, customer reports of poor service quality may lead to employee perceptions of a negative service climate.

In support of the customer → employee perspective, Ryan, Schmit, and Johnson (1996) found that customer satisfaction over time was significantly related to employee perceptions, but that the reverse was not true. In this study, Ryan et al. collected employee and customer data from 142 auto finance company branches for two consecutive years and then examined the cross-correlations. In a model exploring the Time 1 and Time 2 cross-correlations, they discovered that the effects of customer satisfaction at Time 1 on employee experiences at Time 2 was significant, but that the results linking employee data at Time 1 to customer data at Time 2 was not.

In other words, their analyses suggest that the causal arrow runs from customers to employees rather than the reverse. Ryan et al. (1996) offer some intriguing possible reasons why this might occur. First, they suggested that, in the company where the data were collected, customer satisfaction is a very strong emphasis and data on customer satisfaction are known. In such a case, they argue, it is reasonable that knowledge of customer data has a long-term effect on employees. Second, they offered the same explanation as did Schneider et al. (1998; see below) for why reciprocity characterizes the employee-customer linkage over time: Customer contact in service jobs brings the employees and customers not only physically close, but psychologically close as well. Third, they suggested that, at least in the organization studied, higher levels of customer contact meant more customer problems and greater employee exposure to dissatisfied customers.

To shed additional light on the issue of causality, Schneider et al. (1998) used causal modeling techniques to examine the relationship between employee service climate perceptions and customer perceptions of service quality in bank branches. Employee perceptions of service climate were measured in 1990 and 1992, and customer perceptions of service quality were measured for the same time periods. Using

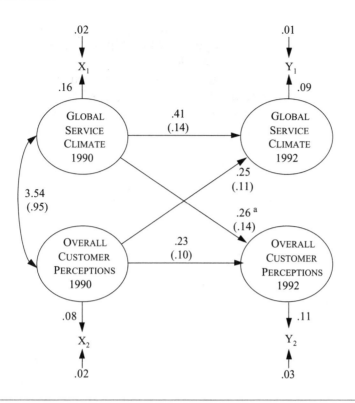

Figure 4.1   Reciprocal Employee-Customer Relationships

NOTE: These are unstandardized coefficients; only significant ones are presented (p < .05). Standard errors appear in parenthesis. a: p = .06

SOURCE: From Schneider et al, (1998). Copyright © 1998 by American Psychological Association.

cross-lagged panel analysis, Schneider et al. examined the question of whether employee perceptions in 1990 caused customer perceptions in 1992 to a greater or lesser extent than customer perceptions in 1990 caused employee perceptions in 1992. The structural equation model analyzed to answer this question is shown in Figure 4.1.

The model presented in Figure 4.1 fits the data well, with a CFI of 0.93 and a BBNFI of 0.94.[6] Furthermore, three of the four paths in the model were significant ($p < 0.05$), and the fourth approached significance with a p value of 0.06. In other words, rather than supporting a service climate → customer perceptions or a customer perceptions → service climate perspective, Figure 4.1 supports a reciprocal relationship of service climate ↔ customer perceptions of service quality.

Given that there had been previous support for both causal directions, the finding of a reciprocal relationship was not surprising. The physical closeness of service employees and customers is essentially reflected in a psychological closeness—they share experiences and influence each other. Indeed, Bowen (1983) suggested that customers are a great source of information for employees about how they, the employees, are doing and how well their organization is performing. Furthermore, Bowen suggested that customers can in fact be more important than internal managers and bosses with regard to directing (leading) employees, conceptualizing employees as "substitutes for leaders" (Kerr & Jermeir, 1978). We are unaware of research that has tested this idea directly, but we are aware of one study showing that employees attempt to keep customers from gaining the upper hand when both parties are in a service relationship (Rafaeli, 1989). The metatheme in this regard concerns the impact that customers can have on employees and the way employees eventually come to see their working world.

Linkage Research as Validation of Employee Surveys

The research linking employee perceptions to customer perceptions has been very important to both the services literature and the organizational literature in general. In the realm of services, the linkage research allowed organizations to see that steps they took internally to encourage their employees to deliver quality service actually affected the service that customers reported they received. In other words, the research provided evidence as to the practical usefulness of implementing a climate for service in an organization.

The linkage research was also important from the general perspective of organizational research. Linking customer perceptions to employee perceptions essentially validated the perceptions of employees about their organization. At the time the original linkage research was conducted, employee surveys were often regarded as being of low practical utility. They were typically considered to be measures of job satisfaction or morale, and these employee attitudes were not usually considered to be linked strongly to employee behaviors other than turnover or absenteeism. Most organizations gave employees little say or decision-making power in their work, and employee input was not highly valued.

However, with the advent of linkage research, it now is quite clear that employees' reports on internal organizational functioning and processing are in turn related to customer assessments of their experiences with the organization. Customer reports about the organization essentially backed up what the employees were saying, and this lent credence to the employee reports. Thus the linkage results reveal the fact that employee perceptions are valid, that they represent not only the reality of employees, but are also reflected significantly in the reality of customers. These findings support the notion that employees are potentially useful sources of information for organizational improvement and change, a topic we will address in some detail later.

Summary

A lot of information about organizational climate, service climate, and linkage concepts and methods has been presented in a fairly compact space. To summarize, the main ideas presented here are as follows:

1. People in organizations perceive meaning in the patterns of what happens to and around them (i.e., the policies, practices, and procedures and what gets rewarded, supported, and expected).

2. The meaning attached to these experiences constitutes a gestalt or a whole that can be of strategic importance when focused on important organizational behaviors, like service quality.

3. The service-focused gestalt experienced by employees can be called a service climate, and this climate has components ranging from management service practices to active attention to customers to the degree to which internal activities by others facilitate service delivery to customers.

4. The service climate experienced by employees is reflected in customer experiences and customer satisfaction.

5. Customer experiences and customer satisfaction appear to be reciprocally related over time to employee climate perceptions.

6. Documentation of the validity of employee perceptions has implications for the way employees are conceptualized in models of organizational effectiveness.

Creating a Service Climate

In the next section, our goal is to take the results presented above regarding service climate and show how these results can be parsed for hints about practical implications. Thus, while neither one of us can claim to be experts in organizational change, we think the diagnostic information generated through a climate approach to understanding organizations can be useful. In other words, once we know that employee perceptions have validity with regard to customer experiences, we can capitalize on the information provided by employees— and on other information we can acquire—to make the changes that might enhance both employee and customer experiences. In what follows, we will take a less abstract and less holistic view of the climate topic, and focus on some more concrete ideas that are more suitable for research in this area. To our minds, these are questions that are both conceptually interesting and practically meaningful.

Role of the Leader

A good place to begin might be with the topic of leadership, since that is where the research on climate in general began. In Lewin, Lippitt, and White's (1939) seminal climate study, differences in climates were attributed to leaders who treated their subordinates with different leadership styles. Given that leaders have the capacity to impact their subordinates' atmosphere, the role of organizational leadership with respect to service climate bears some examination. The role of leaders (i.e., top management) in establishing a service climate is (a) to espouse service-oriented values to employees, (b) to design organizational policies, practices, and procedures that are consistent with these values, and (c) to ensure reward and recognition go to those who most fully implement the policies and procedures to achieve the service vision. The policies, practices, and procedures under which employees operate are the tangible evidence they have about whether the organization's leaders actually believe in the value of quality service or if they are just "talking the talk." Recall Lytle et al.'s (1998) service climate survey item: "There is a true commitment to service, not just lip service." When the policies, practices, and procedures that are created are consistent with the value of delivering quality service, a positive service climate can be the result.

In the larger research literature on leadership, perhaps the most salient conceptualization for present purposes is the one known as the *path-goal theory* of leadership (Evans, 1970; House & Dessler, 1974; House & Mitchell, 1974). The theory proposes that the major job of a leader is to clarify the behaviors (paths) required by followers for them to attain goals or outcomes that are valent (valued) to them. The paths clarified should be those that are most useful to the goals of organizational effectiveness, thus facilitating both organizational and individual outcome attainment and satisfaction. With regard to service, in particular, path-goal theory would propose that the path to goal attainment would be service quality behaviors and that valent outcomes would be tied to such behaviors. The challenge for a leader is, of course, to clarify and facilitate the paths most likely to promote service quality experiences for customers—and then reward followers engaging in those behaviors with valent outcomes.

Foundations of Service Climate

The model of leadership just presented—as well as just about all other theories of leadership—appears to be essentially context free. That is, the situation in which the leader behaves has not been the focus of as much research and theory as have the behaviors in which the leader should engage. Path-goal theory has been an exception to this, especially in the form it took with House and Dessler (1974), where they proposed that the leader must first assess the situation to determine the kinds of behaviors that are most likely to be effective there. What path-goal theory and other leadership theories do not do a good job of is identifying the role of the leader in *creating* a context for him- or herself and his or her followers. For example, in Fiedler's (1967, 1995) contingency theory, the situation is critical for the leader's choice of behavior, but important facets of that situation are seen to be out of the leader's control. Or, consider Hersey and Blanchard's (1969, 1982) situational leadership theory, which proposes that different leader behaviors are likely to be effective depending on the maturity of the followers. Again, the context (i.e., follower maturity) is assessed, but is seen to be outside the leader's control. We could go on, but the point is that, even with contingency theories of leadership, the context is seen as something that exists and must be taken into account, but not something to be manipulated or changed by the leader.

An alternative scheme is to think about leaders as those who *create* situations. That is, leaders can be conceptualized in terms of the specific actions they take with regard to the establishment of a particular kind of climate. However, before a service climate can be established, a foundation for such a climate must be built. In other words, it would be difficult for a leader to establish a climate for service in isolation from other support systems and procedures—we would argue that just directly focusing on service delivery is difficult unless there exist conditions facilitating such a focus. We propose, then, that an organization's climate for service—or climate for any strategic initiative, for that matter—must rest on what has been called in earlier writings a "climate for work facilitation" (Schneider et al., 1998). A climate for work facilitation is essentially employees' summary sense of how well they are supported in their efforts to do their work. It refers to (a) efforts made to remove obstacles to work (Burke et al., 1996; Schoorman & Schneider, 1988), (b) supervisory behaviors (e.g., giving feedback and sharing information; Schneider & Bowen, 1985), and (c) human resources management (HRM) policies (Schneider & Bowen, 1993).

The basic idea captured by a climate for work facilitation is that leaders in an organization must not only encourage and push employees to deliver quality service (as with a climate for service), but also *enable* employees to deliver quality service. For example, it does little good to reward employees for delivering quality service if they lack the supplies they need to do so. Burke et al. (1992) offered some evidence, for example, that employees perceive a climate for work facilitation as separate from a climate for service. They showed that employees' perceptions of their work environment could be modeled in terms of a "concern for employees" factor (similar to our climate for work facilitation) and a "concern for customers" factor (what we call a climate for service).

Another element of a service climate's foundation is that of internal service. We briefly discussed internal service earlier, where we indicated that employees must receive good service from other areas in the organization in order to deliver quality service to customers (Grönroos, 1990; Heskett, Sasser, & Hart, 1990; Reynoso & Moores, 1995). Hallowell and Schlesinger (2000), in the context of the service profit chain, define internal service quality as "the quality of services that employees and managers receive from an organization to enable them to do their jobs" (p. 209). In other words, employees within an organization should deliver service to each other as they would deliver service to external customers. All recipients of service should be considered customers—whether they are internal customers, in the form of other employees or areas of the organization, or external customers. But who will ensure that this will happen? This is another job for leadership in facilitating the conditions (i.e., in providing the context) in which the desired behaviors can occur.

When internal service is high, it serves two functions. First, it emphasizes the importance of service in general, which should serve to strengthen the organization's service climate. In addition, good internal service is another enabling factor that allows employees to deliver quality service to external customers. Thus, as mentioned above,

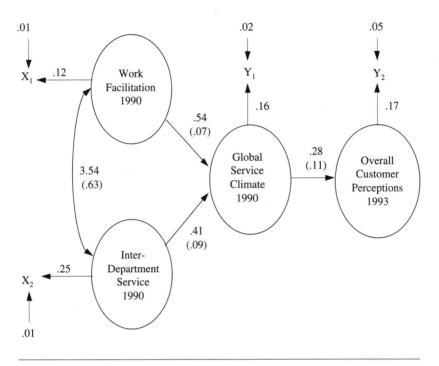

Figure 4.2   Model Linking Foundation Issues, Service Climate, and Customer Perceptions

SOURCE: From Schneider et al. (1998). Copyright © 1998 by American Psychological Association.

internal service is a second foundation element in building a climate for service.

The idea that a climate for service rests on a foundation of work facilitation and internal service was presented earlier. The model that we presented then was empirically tested by Schneider et al. (1998) on a sample of 132 bank branches. The results are presented above in Figure 4.2.

The model presented in Figure 4.2 depicts the foundation issues discussed above as preceding a climate for service, which in turn leads to customer perceptions of service quality. The climate for work facilitation idea was represented as Work Facilitation. Specifically, this variable reflected four aspects of work facilitation: (1) the quality of leadership provided by managers, (2) the extent to which employees participated in decisions that affected their work and their customers, (3) the quality of the technical and computer support that employees received, and

Table 4.6   Dimensions for a Measure of Internal Service

Helpfulness
Promptness
Communication
Tangibles
Professionalism
Reliability
Confidentiality
Flexibility
Preparedness
Consideration

SOURCE: Based on Reynoso and Moores (1995).

(4) the adequacy of the training that employees received for doing their jobs. If a service firm leader were looking for a set of topics deserving attention, this list might be a useful place to begin.

Obviously, the specific items used to assess these issues would be specific to different businesses, but the issues would seem to generalize across settings. The question then becomes one of who is responsible for ensuring that training, participation, and resources will be optimal for employees. If these are not good task requirements for leaders and managers, what are?

But Figure 4.2 also shows that a service climate rests on the internal service foundation. Thus the data reveal that it is not sufficient to pay attention to only the "work facilitation" issues shown in Figure 4.2, but that employees in each department or area of a business must also have the sense that they can count on other areas of the firm. Reynoso and Moores (1995) developed a measure of the internal service construct that yielded 10 separable dimensions, presented in Table 4.6.[7]

In Schneider et al. (1998), the internal service construct was labeled Inter-Department Service, and it was designed to capture the service quality delivered to employees by other areas within the organization. Their measure had 10 items like those shown in Table 4.7.

The reason we go into considerable detail on this issue is that, in the Schneider et al. (1998) project, employee responses to the Inter-Department Service scale alone predicted customer reports of service quality. Thus not only does internal service seem to be a foundation issue for a climate for service, but it also seems to be directly related to customer experiences. One certainly might surmise that receiving the service one needs to serve others facilitates the delivery of the same—and thus generates more positive experiences for end-user customers.

Table 4.7 Sample Items Comprising a Measure of Internal Service Like Those Used in Schneider et al. (1998)

Respondents are asked to choose another area in their business on which they most depend to deliver service quality to customers. After indicating that area (from a provided list), they then rate employees in that area on each item.

Their helpfulness

Their job-related knowledge

Their overall service quality

Their responsiveness

Their keeping of promises they make

Their ability to solve problems we have

Their getting things done right the first time

Their cooperativeness

SOURCE: Copyright © 2003 by Personnel Research Associates, Inc. Used by permission. Not to be duplicated or used without explicit written permission.

The model presented in Figure 4.2 fits the data well, using both (a) work facilitation and (b) internal service as foundations for (c) service climate, with (d) subsequent customer experiences. All of the paths were significant, and the model was characterized by a CFI of 0.98 and a BBNFI of 0.97. Furthermore, support for the model was gathered from testing an alternative model. When the position of the foundation issues and climate for service were reversed, such that Global Service Climate preceded Work Facilitation and Inter-Department Service, the model fit the data significantly less well. In addition, it should be noted that the model supports previous linkage research in finding a significant relationship between service climate and customer perceptions of service quality over a three-year time lag.

These findings and the details shown in Table 4.6 and Table 4.7 reveal a set of attributes that a manager could use as a wedge in arranging between-department mutual service contracts or agreements. That is, if Area A depends on Area B for serving customers, perhaps Areas A and B can agree on what reasonable service would be and literally sign contracts to fulfill those agreements. In this way, the details could be worked out and a mutual understanding would emerge so that Area A might maximally meet the needs of its internal customers.

In thinking about internal service, it is important to keep in mind the vast array of dependencies that exists in organizations. Certainly, frontline employees need support in delivering service to end-user customers. However, even those backroom employees providing this support need service from other areas themselves. Lovelock (2001, pp. 492–493) does an excellent job of identifying some of the many other ways intraorganizational coordination can be enhanced:

- Transfers and cross-training of employees and managers—here, both employees and managers actually experience the work and challenges of others with whom they interact.

- Creating cross-functional task forces—using people in different jobs and at different points in the chain to the customer to tackle specific challenges or problems so that the eventual practice developed has benefited from diverse sources of information.

- Integrating the organization's personnel with the personnel in the organization of the customers—here, employees of a firm literally work in the customers' firm to enhance specific knowledge about the challenges faced by the customer.

- Installation of corporate intranets—these provide up-to-date information on the organization with regard to sales, customer satisfaction, and other changes and accomplishments, as well as instant access to required knowledge.

There is not a lot of research on the effects of these internal service issues with regard to customer satisfaction, but it is a topic that could profit from further conceptual thinking and data.

Human Resources Management

The foundation issues that we have discussed—work facilitation and internal service—are only intended to serve as a foundation for a climate for service; they are necessary but not sufficient conditions. Obviously, other issues determine service climate and service quality delivered to customers. Another equally relevant issue, somewhat touched on by the training items in the Work Facilitation measure, concerns the broad issue of HRM. The extent to which HRM practices, policies, and procedures are designed to encourage and allow employees to deliver quality service is a primary influence over how employees develop their sense of the service climate of their organization. That said, it is essential to remember that HRM is only one determinant of perceptions of service climate. Attaching too much importance to it is what Schneider and Bowen (1995) have spoken of as the "HRM trap."

Of course, we would agree that HRM practices focused on service quality facilitate the development of a service climate! Prior to outlining some hypotheses about what these HRM issues might be, though, we want to digress for a bit and discuss the issue of what has come to be called "strategic human resources management" (see, for example, Wright & Snell, 1998). While there has been a variety of approaches to conceptualizing and studying this issue (e.g., Lepak & Snell, 1999), the basic issue fundamentally concerns the hypothesized strategic advantage of approaching the human component of organizations as if it matters. For example, in the excellent research accomplished by Huselid (1995), organizations found to be performing in the marketplace at superior levels are shown to have more active HRM practices in place.

We agree that organizations are likely to be more effective when their HRM practices are more in keeping with the best practices in this arena. However, we think of this approach to strategic HRM as a generic approach: Do HRM better. In the present case—service quality—we think of strategic HRM as doing HRM better so that service quality delivered to customers is enhanced. In this nongeneric mode, HRM has a specific focus—service—and HRM now becomes specifically, rather than generically, strategic.

The point, of course, is that organizations tell employees what is important through the practices it has in place and, more specifically, the focus of those practices. If service is strategically important, one way employees get this message is through what they encounter in the way of HRM practices.

What are the HRM practices and policies that can contribute to a service climate? As with the dimensions of service quality and the dimensions of service climate, it is uncertain that there is a universal set of service-oriented HRM practices that will be effective across all settings and organizations (Bowen, Schneider, & Kim, 2000). Thus each organization attempting to establish a service climate must determine the specific practices and policies that are right for it. As will become clear in what follows, a first step in this process might be to consult with the organization's boundary workers—those employees who actually interact with the organization's end-user customers. These might be the tellers in a bank or the salespeople in a department store. Boundary workers are the interface between organizations and their customers and, as such, are in a perfect position to know what may be required for them to be more effective in dealing with those customers. Of course, a second step might be to talk with the organization's customers. We address approaches to dealing with customer data first, and then move on to consultation with employees. In both cases, we frame the issue first with regard to training and then with regard to other HRM practices.

Training. In the literature on training, the key issue is to identify through needs analysis what actually requires training attention (Goldstein & Ford, 2002). Needs analysis has a number of formal components to it, and in the world of service these formal components require data from both employees and customers. As discussed earlier with regards to linkage research, there is a psychological closeness between service employees and their customers. We mentioned that this closeness might derive in part from customers telling employees about their service experiences with the organization. Employee reports about what they know customers desire from them could be a crucial element in the design of training practices within the organization.

In fact, there is independent research evidence that the range of issues employees are aware of that require attention is very large. Chung and Schneider (2002), for example, asked employees in focus groups to tell them about what they felt customers expected them to do to meet customer expectations. In three focus groups of telephone salespeople from a property casualty insurance company, the employees generated 89 separable customer expectations of them! Table 4.8 presents just 10 of these, providing an idea of the range and complexity of the information employees have about what customers expect—and perhaps a start in the design of appropriate training programs.

Another obvious source of potential information as input into training would be data directly from customers. For example, we (Benjamin Schneider & Amy Nicole Salvaggio, personal communication, March 14, 2002) have some unpublished research on customers using a variation of the procedure we called *driver analysis* in Chapter 2. (Recall that driver analysis is a statistical procedure that can be used for determining which facets of service quality appear to contribute the most to overall customer satisfaction.) The project was conducted in the credit card industry, using data from the merchants who accept credit cards.

A specific interest in the project was the quality of service that merchants experienced when they called the credit card service center representatives with a query or a problem. Merchants were called as a follow-up to their own calls to the service center and asked a series of questions about the call. At the end of the follow-up telephone survey, merchants were asked to rate the overall quality of the service they

Table 4.8   Employee Reports on Customer Expectations of Them

---

Customers expect

1. Quotes from me in less than ten minutes.
2. No more than one hold per phone contact.
3. Me to probe them to find out what information they want to know.
4. Me to keep accurate and up-to-date records.
5. Me to attach additional notes or explanations to what I send them, even though I have already explained it over the phone.
6. Me to have knowledge of other companies' policies and procedures.
7. Me to have knowledge of motor vehicle registration requirements.
8. Me to remain polite even when they are rude.
9. Me to explain each type of coverage they have or might buy in detail.
10. Me to have knowledge of different kinds of cars, the different cars' safety records, and what options come with these cars.

SOURCE: Adapted from Chung (1996).

received when they originally called. In addition, they were asked about the specific facets of the service they received during their original call:

- whether the length of the call was too long, too short, or as expected;
- whether the time it took to resolve the question/problem was shorter, longer, or as expected;
- whether the representatives knew how to help them;
- whether the representative was professional; and
- whether the representative with whom they spoke took responsibility for resolving the inquiry.

Replies to these specific questions were correlated with the general question concerning overall service quality, and these correlations revealed that the most important facets of service quality concerned representatives being knowledgeable, professional, and taking responsibility; the least important facets concerned the length of the call and the time it took to resolve the inquiry. These results seemed to generalize across a wide variety of reasons for the merchants making the call in the first place (e.g., questions about a new account, payments, supplies). The organization now had evidence it could use in designing training for the representatives: Worry more about training for complete knowledge and professionalism than for speed.

Training is not the only element that seems to matter with regard to the HRM signals organizations send about the importance of service quality. For example, Schneider, Wheeler, and Cox (1992) also found that the HRM areas of hiring procedures, performance feedback, and internal equity of compensation were all positively correlated with employee reports of the degree to which their organization emphasized service (i.e., the extent to which the organization had a "service passion"). What this means is that organizations in which these HRM activities are at a high level are also organizations where employees report that service quality is highly emphasized.

Selection. In addition to training, an organization that wants to send the message that service quality is important might examine the service orientation of the people they hire. For example, organizations with a strong service climate might pay more attention to hiring employees that have service-oriented personalities. Frei and McDaniel (1998) discuss the implications of hiring boundary workers in customer-contact positions on the basis of personality, and they provide a meta-analysis of four measures that have been used to make such hiring decisions.[8]

Frei and McDaniel (1998) did indeed find that personality-based measures of service orientation reveal consistent predictive validity coefficients with supervisors' ratings of employees' performance. In fact, their results are surprisingly strong, with an average true validity coefficient of 0.50 across diverse samples of 6,945 service workers. Analyses of the measures suggest that the personality facets being assessed in these measures are Agreeableness, Extraversion, and Emotional Stability—three of the five factors that constitute the "Big Five" model of personality (Costa & McCrae, 1985). Hough and R. Schneider (1996) suggest that the service-oriented personality can be characterized as "resilient and coolheaded; cautious, planful, and thoughtful; willing to cooperate and defer to others; willing to adhere to strict standards of conduct; and interested in helping others and providing them service" (p. 61; also see Lytle et al., 1998).

To our knowledge, there is no research on the degree to which *customers* report superior service when they are served by employees who score high on a service-orientation personality measure. That is, the research to date has validated the personality measures only against supervisor ratings. In addition, there is no research on whether organizations that use such measures have stronger service climates than those that do not use such measures to make hiring decisions. Such cross-level research would seem to be very useful, but we would expect that using such measures for hiring without doing many of the other things we recommend would not improve a service climate much. Thus it takes more than hiring service-oriented people to make a service climate.

There are, of course, selection procedures other than personality tests that could be used for selecting service workers. One procedure we particularly like is the use of simulations, because they provide an opportunity for potential employees to experience what the job is actually like. Simulations might require potential service employees to handle rude customers (played by role players), interact with role players who have complaints, utilize the various information technologies required by the particular job, and so forth. Some firms administer such simulations by telephone to make hiring decisions for jobs that are handled by telephone (e.g., service center customer service representatives). During simulations, participants' behaviors are judged by trained observers. A strong signal about the importance of service quality could be sent by placing those who make the hiring decisions in the roles of judges. This would emphasize how important specific kinds of service-oriented behaviors are when considering new hires.

Performance Appraisal and Compensation. Another area of HRM to which organizations might pay attention in establishing a service climate is their performance appraisal systems (Schneider, 1991). That is, the adage of "what gets measured gets attended to" should apply to organizations attempting to establish a climate that encourages the delivery of quality service. If employees are rated on their service delivery or customer orientation, it is much more likely that employees will begin to pay attention to these kinds of issues. The question is, Who should be providing the ratings?

Recent developments in performance appraisal for managers and executives concern what has come to be called "360-degree feedback" (see Tornow & London, 1998). The idea in 360-degree feedback is that managers and executives are appraised from multiple vantage points—colleagues and peers, subordinates, clients, and superiors. To our knowledge, though, few evaluations—and few studies of 360-degree feedback—have actually included input from external clients or customers. While many companies monitor their service workers have all made phone calls that are "being recorded for quality control purposes"), the monitors are either hired experts or internal supervisors, not customers. It would certainly make a strong statement about the importance of service quality in an organization if boundary workers and managers were evaluated by end-user customers.

Building customer input into the regular appraisals of employees at all levels is one step toward emphasizing the importance of service, but employees are much more likely to appreciate the importance of this if it is tied to their pay. In general, people will devote more time and effort to an area in which they are being evaluated if their evaluations are in turn tied to their compensation (see Rynes & Gerhart, 2000). Thus an organization's compensation practices and policies can be designed to encourage certain types of actions, such as service orientation. Employees might receive money or other forms of recognition if they receive positive comments from customers, or receive a bonus if their service orientation rating is above a given level.

Of course, employees must be trained in areas in which they are to be evaluated and compensated, emphasizing the need for the HRM functions of an organization to be in alignment. HRM practices, such as hiring, performance appraisal, compensation, and training, can all take on a service focus in efforts to develop a service climate. Of course, a theme of fair play should run through all HRM practices and policies in an organization. For example, employees might consider it unfair to evaluate them and compensate them on service delivery if they received no training in this area. Perhaps employees would interpret as unfair a hiring practice based on personality unless the reasoning behind the practice, and empirical evidence to support it, were presented to them.

While treating employees fairly is a noble goal in and of itself, it is also important for its implications for customers. By treating employees fairly through HRM systems, employees are more likely to treat customers fairly in turn. Such treatment should favorably affect customer attitudes and perceptions of service quality (Bowen, Gilliland, & Folger, 1999; Masterson, 2001), again reflecting the psychological closeness of employees and customers of service organizations.

Market Segmentation as an HRM Issue. In our discussions of service climate to this point, we have typically referred to the idea of establishing an atmosphere within the organization that encourages and supports employees in their efforts to deliver quality service. However, recall from Chapter 2 that the *meaning* of quality service may be different for different firms—even firms in the same industry. Thus the idea that customers within an industry (e.g., the food industry) can hold different expectations for service quality falls under the topic of market segmentation. *Market segmentation* refers to the idea that customers are not all interchangeable with each other, but rather that certain groups will want and expect things that other groups will not. For example, customers who enter a fast-food restaurant likely have different expectations and place different demands on the organization than do customers who enter a luxurious, five-star restaurant. The message for organizations is that they must determine the market segment to which they wish to cater, and establish their HRM policies and practices—and the resultant service climate—accordingly. Essentially, the market segment an organization chooses is a reflection of its strategic focus (Bowen et al., 2000).

Given this logic, we would argue that organizations must create service climates that have different priorities—and establish different kinds of HRM practices and policies—in order to provide service quality in their market segment. That is, organizations must create and maintain a service climate that is appropriate for the market segment in which they wish to compete. Chung (1996) examined this idea empirically. She hypothesized that aspects of HRM practices, such as pay for performance, performance appraisal, and training, should emphasize segment-relevant attributes and that, if they did, customers of those units would report superior satisfaction with service. For example, fast-food restaurants should train for speed of delivery, appraise employees on speed of delivery, and compensate employees based on speed. In contrast, she proposed that in the white-linen restaurants she studied, training should be on responsiveness to requests rather than purely on speed, that appraisals should focus on empathy and assurance, and that compensation should emphasize these more social psychological facets of service. Chung's results did support these hypotheses. Customer satisfaction was higher when employees described their organization's HRM practices as consistent with their market segments.

As another example of fitting HRM practices and service climate development to particular market segments, consider Bowen and Lawler's (1992, 1995) contingency approach to employee empowerment. These authors proposed that employee empowerment—employees' power to act autonomously and make decisions on their own—might only be necessary in organizations with customers who demand highly personalized service (i.e., the market segment that demands "tender loving care," TLC). When customers are demanding only efficiency, complicated and expensive hiring, training, and compensation systems may not be worth the investment. As Bowen et al. (2000) stated,

If the targeted market segment values inexpensive, speedy service—not TLC—then Levitt's (1972; 1976) production-line approach of procedurally-driven, low employee discretion jobs might be the best fit for that specific segment. Alternatively, if the strategy is to compete on the provision of differentiated, TLC service, then designing an HRM mix to empower employees to provide customized service to customers would be appropriate. (p. 450)

This idea of designing service climates—and HRM policies—on the basis of customer demands is essentially a reflection of what has been called "customer-driven employee performance" (Bowen & Waldman, 1999). This perspective holds that employee requirements (e.g., evaluation standards) and desired behaviors should be defined in terms of customer requirements. In other words, "The customer is the ultimate judge of success and the one most likely to guide employees in the proper direction and to prompt change in response to changing customer expectations" (Bowen et al., 2000, p. 448).

Conclusion

The research outlined early in this chapter emphasized the idea that in the world of service delivery attention to the psychology of the work environment for employees could be important. The logic was that, in a world where intangibles in the delivery process can be the essence of the service and where employees and customers are in continual interaction, the "message" employees have in their heads about what is important will dictate behavior. We used the term *climate* to capture the sense of the generic environment and the term *service climate* to emphasize the thought that an organization can have many foci but that, in the world of service delivery, an important focus (if not the most important focus) would be service delivery quality. When the manager cannot be there to oversee every behavior, when once the service delivery process begins it completely unfolds, when quality of delivery cannot be checked prior to delivery, then what is in the atmosphere will determine behavior. We summarized a lot of research on what has come to be called *linkage research*, revealing that in fact employee reports on the service climate of their setting is consistently and significantly related to both customer evaluations of service quality and customer satisfaction.

In the latter part of the chapter, the issue of how to create a service climate attracted our attention. The logic here and as revealed in the various measures of service climate we presented and discussed was that there is no silver bullet—no one thing—that organizations can do to create the service climate. The leader must focus on service quality, reward systems and performance management systems, and training must all emphasize the importance of delivering superior service. In addition, not just anyone, we argued, will be able to fill the roles of service delivery—there are important individual differences in service orientation, too, to which attention should be paid. More specifically, we said, an organization's HRM practices and policies should be designed to create a service climate that is consistent with the market segment the organization wishes to serve.

In the final chapter, we will integrate this emphasis on HRM issues with marketing and operations management approaches to suggest a set of important issues that might benefit from more integrated future research.

Notes

1. Although our treatment of organizational climate may seem at times to stray from the topic of service quality, we felt a general review of climate issues was important for understanding service climate research.

2. This is our formal composition model, the direct composition model, for relating psychological and organizational climate (Chan, 1998). Composition models basically delineate the functional connection between phenomena that capture the same content area but that are represented at different levels of analysis. This explicit specification of relationships helps provide precision in defining what the constructs mean at different levels, which is in turn beneficial in testing hypotheses.

3. Do organizations have *a* climate—or do they have *many* climates? (The same question has arisen in the culture literature.) Organizations may have multiple climates focused on multiple aspects of organizational functioning or on the needs of multiple stakeholders (White, Paul, & Schneider, 1999). Simultaneously, however, it is also conceivable that an organization might have a superordinate climate that pervades all aspects of organizational functioning, such as a climate for fairness.

4. This statistical procedure assists researchers in clustering survey items into sets of items that are relatively highly correlated with one another, but not highly correlated with the items in other clusters.

5. Schneider et al. (1980) merely ran an ANOVA—the equivalent of an ICC(2)—to defend aggregation to the branch level of analysis, although one could not get away with doing only this today. Schneider and Bowen (1985) opted for r_{wg}, arguing, at that time, that the real challenge in research of this kind is to reveal that people within a setting agree on what that setting is.

6. These statistics are indicators of the extent to which a hypothesized set of relationships actually captures the data submitted for analysis (see, for example, Bentler, 1995). Fit indices close to 1.00 are indicators of good fit, so the present indices suggest good fit of the model to the data.

7. These dimensions were generated from 37 items via principal components factor analysis with oblique rotation. Recall from Chapter 2 that the oblique rotational procedure yields factors that are correlated with each other, in contrast to orthogonal rotation, which yields factors that are uncorrelated with each other. Note that Reynoso and Moores (1995) derived their measure of internal service much like Parasuraman, Zeithaml, and Berry developed SERVQUAL.

8. Meta-analysis (also called *validity generalization*) is a statistical procedure for summarizing research that has been conducted on a similar topic. Meta-analysis looks at the sampling distribution of results generated from multiple studies, and asks (a) if the pattern has the kind of normal distribution one would expect (some correlation coefficients are high, some are low, and most are bunched in the middle) and (b) if the mean of that distribution of correlation coefficients is statistically significant. Prior to the development of the validity generalization procedure, it was assumed that different measures of similar constructs, and the same measures used in different settings, always required extensive study prior to use in making hiring decisions. Validity generalization research, although hardly without controversy, has yielded the following insights: (a) the conduct of test validity research on small samples is a bad idea, because the results on small samples can be highly variable; and (b) validity generalization procedures can reveal cross-situational and cross-measure consistency that suggests the generalizability of validity—as the name of the procedure suggests (Guion, 1998). Guion (1998) provides an excellent introduction to validity generalization.

References

Bartko, J. J. (1976). On various intraclass correlation reliability coefficients. *Psychological Bulletin, 83*, 762–765.

Bentler, P. M. (1995). *EQS structural equations program manual.* Encino, CA: Multivariate Software, Inc.

Bliese, P. D. (2000).Within-group agreement, non-indpendence, and reliability: Implications for data aggregation and analysis. In K. J. Klein & S. W. J. Kozlowski (Eds.), *Multilevel theory, research, and methods in organizations* (pp. 349–381). San Francisco: Jossey-Bass.

Bowen, D. E. (1983). *Customers as substitutes for leadership in service organizations.* Unpublished doctoral dissertation, Michigan State University.

Bowen, D. E., Gilliland, S., & Folger, R. (1999). HRM and service fairness: How being fair with employees spills over to customers. *Organizational Dynamics, 27*, 7–23.

Bowen, D. E., & Lawler, E. E. (1992). The empowerment of service workers: What, why, how, and when. *Sloan Management Review, 33*(3), 31–39.

Bowen, D. E., & Lawler, E. E. (1995). Empowerment of service employees. *Sloan Management Review, 36*(4), 73–84.

Bowen, D. E., Schneider, B., & Kim, S. S. (2000). Shaping service culture through strategic human resource management. In T. A. Swartz & D. Iacobucci (Eds.), *Handbook of services marketing and management* (pp. 439–454). Thousand Oaks, CA: Sage.

Bowen, D. E., & Waldman, D. A. (1999). Customer-driven employee performance. In D. R. Ilgen & E. A. Pulakos (Eds.), *The changing nature of performance: Implications for staffing, motivation, and development* (pp. 154–191). San Francisco: Jossey-Bass.

Burke, M., Borucki, C., & Hurley, A. (1992). Reconceptualizing psychological climate in a retail service environment: A multiple stakeholder perspective. *Journal of Applied Psychology, 77*, 717–729.

Burke, M., Rapinski, M., Dunlap, W., & Davison, H. (1996). Do situational variables act as substantive causes of relationships between individual difference variables? Two large-scale tests of common cause models. *Personnel Psychology, 49*, 573–598.

Chan, D. (1998). Functional relations among constructs in the same content domain at different levels of analysis: A typology of composition models. *Journal of Applied Psychology, 83*(2), 234–246.

Chung, B. G. (1996). *Focusing HRM strategies toward service market segments: A three-factor model.* Unpublished doctoral dissertation, University of Maryland at College Park.

Chung, B. G., & Schneider, B. (2002). Serving multiple masters: Role conflict experienced by service employees. *Journal of Services Marketing, 16*, 70–85.

Costa, P. T., & McRae, R. R. (1985). *The NEO Personality Inventory manual.* Odessa, FL: Psychological Assessment Resources.

Dansereau, F., Jr., & Alutto, J. A. (1990). Level-of-analysis issues in climate and culture research. In B. Schneider (Ed.), *Organizational climate and culture* (pp. 193–236). San Francisco: Jossey-Bass.

Evans, M. G. (1970). The effects of supervisory behavior on the path-goal relationship. *Organizational Behavior and Human Performance, 5,* 277–298.

Fiedler, F. E. (1967). *A theory of leadership effectiveness.* New York: McGraw-Hill.

Fiedler, F. E. (1995). Reflections by an accidental theorist. *Leadership Quarterly, 6,* 453–461.

Fitzgerald, L. F., Drasgow, F., Hulin, C. L., Gelfand, M. J., & Magley, V. J. (1997). Antecedents and consequences of sexual harassment in organizations: A test of an integrated model. *Journal of Applied Psychology, 82,* 578–589.

Frei, R. L., & McDaniel, M. A. (1998). Validity of customer service measures on personnel selection: A review of criterion and construct evidence. *Human Performance, 11*(1), 1–27.

George, J. M., & James, L. R. (1993). Personality, affect, and behavior in groups revisited: Comment on aggregation, levels of analysis, and a recent application of within and between analysis. *Journal of Applied Psychology, 78,* 798–804.

Glick, W. H. (1985). Conceptualizing and measuring organizational and psychological climate: Pitfalls in multilevel research. *Academy of Management Review, 10,* 601–616.

Goldstein, I., & Ford, J. K. (2002). *Training in organizations* (4th ed.). Pacific Grove, CA: Wadsworth.

Grönroos, C. (1990). Relationship approach to marketing in service contexts: The marketing and organizational behavior interface. *Journal of Business Research, 20,* 3–11.

Guion, R. M. (1973). A note on organizational climate. *Organizational Behavior and Human Performance, 9,* 120–125.

Guion, R. M. (1998). Assessment, measurement, and prediction for personnel decisions. Mahwah, NJ: Lawrence Erlbaum.

Hallowell, R., & Schlesinger, L. A. (2000). The service profit chain: Intellectual roots, current realities, and future prospects. In T. A. Swartz & D. Iacobucci (Eds.), *Handbook of services marketing and management* (pp. 203–221). Thousand Oaks, CA: Sage.

Hartline, M., & Ferrell, O. (1993). *Contact employees: Relationships among workplace fairness, job satisfaction, and prosocial service behaviors* [Technical Working Paper]. Cambridge, MA: Marketing Science Institute.

Hersey, P., & Blanchard, K. H. (1969). Life cycle theory of leadership. *Training and Development Journal, 23*(5), 26–34.

Hersey, P., & Blanchard, K. H. (1982). Leadership style: Attitudes and behaviors. *Training and Development Journal, 36*(5), 50–52.

Heskett, J. L., Sasser, W. E., Jr., & Hart, C. W. L. (1990). *Breakthrough service.* New York: Free Press.

Heskett, J. L., Sasser, W. E., Jr., & Schlesinger, L. A. (1997). *The service profit chain: How leading companies link profit and growth to loyalty, satisfaction, and value.* New York: Free Press.

Hough, L. M., & Schneider, R. J. (1996). Personality traits, taxonomies, and applications in organizations. In K. R. Murphy (Ed.), *Individual differences and behavior in organizations* (pp. 31–88). San Francisco: Jossey-Bass.

House, R. J., & Dessler, G. (1974). The path-goal theory of leadership: Some post-hoc and a priori tests. In J. G. Hunt & L. L. Larson (Eds.), *Contingency approaches to leadership* (pp. 29–55). Carbondale: Southern Illinois University Press.

House, R. J., & Mitchell, T. R. (1974). Path-goal theory of leadership. *Contemporary Business, 3,* 81–98.

Huselid, M. A. (1995). The impact of human resource management practices on turnover, productivity, and corporate financial performance. *Academy of Management Journal, 38,* 635–672.

James, L. R. (1982). Aggregation bias in estimates of perceptual agreement. *Journal of Applied Psychology, 67,* 219–229.

James, L. R., Demaree, R. G., & Wolf, G. (1984). Estimating within-group interrater reliability with and without response bias. *Journal of Applied Psychology, 69,* 85–98.

James, L. R., James, L. A., & Ashe, D. K. (1990). The meaning of organizations: The role of cognition and values. In B. Schneider (Ed.), *Organizational climate and culture* (pp. 40–84). San Francisco, CA: Jossey-Bass.

James, L. R., & Jones, A. P. (1974). Organizational climate: A review of theory and research. *Psychological Bulletin, 81,* 1096–1112.

Johnson, J. (1996). Linking employee perceptions to customer satisfaction. *Personnel Psychology, 49,* 831–852.

Jones, A. P., & James, L. R. (1979). Psychological climate: Dimensions and relationships of individual and aggregated work environment perceptions. *Organizational Behavior and Human Performance, 23,* 201–250.

Kerr, S., & Jermier, J. M. (1978). Substitutes for leadership: Their meaning and measurement. *Organizational Behavior and Human Performance, 22,* 375–403.

Klein, K. J., & Kozlowski, S. W. J. (2000). *Multilevel theory, research, and methods in organizations: Foundations, extensions, and new directions.* San Francisco: Jossey-Bass.

LaFollette, W. R., & Sims, H. P., Jr. (1975). Is satisfaction redundant with climate? *Organizational Behavior and Human Performance, 10,* 118–144.

Lepak, D. P., & Snell, S. A. (1999). The human resource architecture: Toward a theory of human capital allocation and development. *Academy of Management Review, 24,* 31–48.

Levitt, T. (1972, September–October). Production-line approach to service. *Harvard Business Review,* pp. 41–52.

Levitt, T. (1976, September–October). Industrialization of service. *Harvard Business Review,* pp. 63–74.

Lewin, K., Lippitt, R., & White, R. K. (1939). Patterns of aggressive behavior in experimentally created "social climates." *Journal of Social Psychology, 10,* 271–299.

Lovelock, C. H. (2001). *Services marketing: People, technology, strategy* (4th ed.). Englewood Cliffs, NJ: Prentice-Hall.

Lytle, R. S., Hom, P. W., & Mokwa, M. P. (1998). SERV*OR: A managerial measure of organizational service-orientation. *Journal of Retailing, 74*(4), 455–489.

Martin, J. (1992). *Cultures in organizations: Three perspectives.* New York: Oxford University Press.

Martin, J. (2002). *Organizational culture: Mapping the terrain.* Thousand Oaks, CA: Sage.

Masterson, S. (2001). A trickle-down model of organizational justice: Relating employees' and customers' perceptions of and reactions to fairness. *Journal of Applied Psychology, 86*(4), 594–604.

McGregor, D. M. (1960). *The human side of enterprise.* New York: McGraw-Hill.

Nunnally, J. C., & Bernstein, I. H. (1994). *Psychometric theory.* New York: McGraw-Hill.

Parasuraman, A., Zeithaml, V., & Berry, L. (1985). A conceptual model of service quality and some implications for future research. *Journal of Marketing, 49*(4), 41–50.

Rafaeli, A. (1989). When clerks meet customers: A test of variables related to emotional expression on the job. *Journal of Applied Psychology, 74,* 385–393.

Reynoso, J., & Moores, B. (1995). Towards the measurement of internal service quality. *International Journal of Service Industry Management, 6,* 64–83.

Roberts, K. H., Hulin, C. L., & Rousseau, D. M. (1978). *Developing an interdisciplinary science of organizations.* San Francisco: Jossey-Bass.

Rousseau, D. M. (1985). Issues of level in organizational research: Multi-level and cross-level perspectives. *Research in Organizational Behavior, 7,* 1–37.

Ryan, A., Schmit, M., & Johnson, R. (1996). Attitudes and effectiveness: Examining relations at an organizational level. *Personnel Psychology, 49,* 853–882.

Rynes, S. L., & Gerhart, B. (Eds.). (2000). *Compensation in organizations: Current research and practice.* San Francisco: Jossey-Bass.

Schein, E. H. (1992). *Organizational culture and leadership* (2nd ed.) San Francisco: Jossey-Bass.

Schmit, M. J., & Allscheid, S. P. (1995). Employee attitudes and customer satisfaction: Making theoretical and empirical connections. *Personnel Psychology, 48,* 521–536.

Schneider, B. (1975). Organizational climates: An essay. *Personnel Psychology, 28,* 447–479.

Schneider, B. (1985). Organizational behavior. *Annual Review of Psychology, 36,* 573–611.

Schneider, B. (1987). The people make the place. *Personnel Psychology, 40,* 437–453.

Schneider, B. (1991). Service quality and profits: Can you have your cake and eat it, too? *Human Resources Planning, 14*(2), 151–157.

Schneider, B. (2000). The psychological life of organizations. In N. M. Ashkanasy, C. P. M. Wilderom, & M. F. Peterson (Eds.), *Handbook of organizational culture and climate* (pp. xvii–xxi). Thousand Oaks, CA: Sage.

Schneider, B., Ashworth, S., Higgs, A., & Carr, L. (1996). Design, validity, and use of strategically focused employee attitude surveys. *Personnel Psychology, 49,* 695–705.

Schneider, B., & Bowen, D. E. (1985). Employee and customer perceptions of service in banks: Replication and extension. *Journal of Applied Psychology, 70,* 423–433.

Schneider, B., & Bowen, D. E. (1993). The service organization: Human resources management is crucial. *Organizational Dynamics, 21,* 39–52.

Schneider, B., & Bowen, D. E. (1995). *Winning the service game.* Boston, MA: Harvard Business School Press.

Schneider, B., Bowen, D. E., Ehrhart, M., & Holcombe, K. (2000). The climate for service: Evolution of a construct. In N. M. Ashkanasy, C. P. M. Wilderom, & M. F. Peterson (Eds.), *Handbook of organizational culture and climate* (pp. 21–36). Thousand Oaks, CA: Sage.

Schneider, B., Brief, A. P., & Guzzo, R. A. (1996). Creating a climate and culture for sustainable organizational change. *Organizational Dynamics, 24*(4), 7–19.

Schneider, B., Parkington, J. J., & Buxton, V. M. (1980). Employee and customer perceptions of service in banks. *Administrative Sciences Quarterly, 25,* 252–267.

Schneider, B., & Reichers, A. (1983). On the etiology of climates. *Personnel Psychology, 36,* 19–39.

Schneider, B., & Snyder, R. A. (1975). Some relationships between job satisfaction and organizational climate. *Journal of Applied Psychology, 60,* 318–328.

Schneider, B., Wheeler, J. K., & Cox, J. F. (1992). A passion for service: Using content analysis to explicate service climate themes. *Journal of Applied Psychology, 77*(5), 705–716.

Schneider, B., White, S. S., & Paul, M. C. (1997). Relationship marketing: An organizational perspective. In T. A. Swartz, D. E. Bowen, & S. W. Brown (Eds.), *Advances in services marketing and management* (Vol. 6, pp. 1–22). Greenwich, CT: JAI.

Schneider, B., White, S. S., & Paul, M. C. (1998). Linking service climate and customer perceptions of service quality in banks: Test of a causal model. *Journal of Applied Psychology, 83*(2), 150–163.

Schoorman, D., & Schneider, B. (Eds.). (1988). *Facilitating work effectiveness.* Lexington, MA: Lexington Books.

Tornow, W. W., & London, M. (Eds.). (1998). *Maximizing the value of 360-degree feedback: A process for successful individual and organizational development.* San Francisco: Jossey-Bass.

Trice, H. M., & Beyer, J. M. (1993). *The cultures of work organizations.* Englewood Cliffs, NJ: Prentice-Hall.

Weick, K. E. (1995). *Sensemaking in organizations.* Thousand Oaks, CA: Sage.

White, S., Paul, M., & Schneider, B. (1999, April–May). Building the total service-oriented organization. Fourteenth Annual SIOP Conference, Atlanta, GA.

White, S., & Schneider, B. (2000). Climbing the advocacy ladder: The impact of disconfirmation of service expectations on customers' behavioral intentions. *Journal of Services Research, 2*(3), 240–253.

Wiley, J. W. (1991). Customer satisfaction and employee opinions: A supportive work environment and its financial cost. *Human Resource Planning, 14,* 117–127.

Wright, P. M., & Snell, S. A. (1998). Toward a unifying framework for exploring fit and flexibility in strategic human resource management. *Academy of Management Review, 23,* 756–772.

Yammarino, F. J., & Markham, S. E. (1992). On the application of within and between analysis: Are absence and affect really group-based phenomena? *Journal of Applied Psychology, 77,* 168–176.

Zohar, D. (2000). A group-level model of safety climate: Testing the effect of group climate on microaccidents in manufacturing jobs. *Journal of Applied Psychology, 85,* 587–596.

5

Where Are We and Where Do We Go From Here?

In this chapter, our goal is to integrate what we have learned about service delivery from marketing, operations management (OM), and organizational behavior/human resources management (OB/HRM) perspectives—a daunting challenge, to say the least! First, we present some frameworks that most adequately integrate across the three fields discussed in the book—marketing, OM, and HRM/OB. We feel it important to focus on OB/HR frameworks and models that might be useful were they to introduce service quality issues explicitly into their thinking. We chose strategic HRM and the high-performance work organization as two such vehicles, the former emphasizing HRM and the latter emphasizing OB. Finally, we conclude with some ideas about needed research regardless of the disciplinary background.

We have written the book for OB/HRM students in particular, but our focus in this last chapter on such researchers of the future should not deter future marketing and OM scholars from proceeding. We obviously hope that services marketing and OM students will also profit from the journey. However, these fields are already more open than OB/HRM are to services in particular and to integration across the different disciplines.

In the previous chapters, we have certainly described a number of diverse approaches taken to the study of service quality. We covered topics ranging from product quality to the attributes of service; from manufacturing outlooks on reducing variability in input to production as the key to quality to the variability that customer contact introduces into services; from thinking about service quality from the customer's vantage point to measuring it; and from how organizational design choices influence employee experiences to how those experiences link with customer experiences.

From a strictly OB/HRM perspective, the most important thing we have learned is that customers are a critical part of the organization. We have learned many other things here about customers—how they experience service, how to understand their satisfaction with service, and so forth—and these learnings will be useful as we proceed in this final chapter. However, from the standpoint of the audience for whom we most wrote this book, the important learning is the centrality of customers to service organizations.

In what follows, we first explore in some detail how the fields of marketing, OM, and OB/HRM treat customers and service quality. Then, we outline a series of other lessons we feel we have learned through exploration of these various fields and their approaches to service quality. Finally, we present a set of research goals for the future.

How Customers and Service Are
Viewed in the Different Fields

First-time readers of the literatures represented in our book must be impressed by the amount of attention accorded customers. It certainly becomes clear that customers are as much a part of the service organization as are the employees. Customers participate in the production of their own services, for example, and this and their mere presence have enormous implications for the design of the service organization, the HRM practices used there, and the ways organizational processes must be able to handle the entry, processing, and exit of customers. Thus organizations must be concerned with more than just serving the customer; they must also focus on setting themselves up to manage the customer contact and interaction that service delivery so often entails. There is obviously a vast universe of service topics to be studied—and many people are working on studying them. The question we ask now, though, is, how big is the services universe in different fields?

Let us consider the three fields of marketing, OM, and HRM/OB. How much consideration is specifically given to services in these areas? The answer is that marketing and OM pay considerable attention, while HRM/OB does not. For example, there is a Services Marketing Division of the American Marketing Association, and there are excellent texts available to describe this subfield of marketing (e.g., Lovelock, 2001; Rust, Zahorik, & Keiningham, 1996; Zeithaml & Bitner, 2000). In more general marketing texts, there is also considerable space given to services marketing. For example, Kerin, Berkowitz, Hartley, and Rudelius (2002) devote an entire chapter to the topic of services marketing, and Armstrong and Kotler (2003) discuss marketing strategies for services in some detail (in a chapter shared with product strategies). Of course, one could say that marketing is all about customers, so it is no wonder they emphasize service to customers in services marketing and marketing texts. But they do more than that—several marketing texts actually integrate a variety of the different perspectives we have addressed. That is, services-marketing texts attend not only to marketing, but also to HRM/OB and OM (e.g., Lovelock, 2001; Zeithaml & Bitner, 2000).

A similar attention to service and service delivery is found in OM, where there are excellent texts on OM and service (e.g., Chase, Aquilano, & Jacobs, 1998; Fitzimmons & Fitzimmons, 1994). And, as in marketing, general texts on OM also pay significant attention to services. For example, Krajewski and Ritzman (2002) cover topics such as "Manufacturing and Services: Differences and Similarities" and "Process Management for Services," and Stevenson (2002) boasts that it has an increased emphasis on services over the previous edition.

In OB and HRM, however, there are no texts on services. Moreover, OB and HRM texts give barely any coverage to services, customers, service quality, or service delivery. Even though several early OB-oriented authors conceptualized organizations as open systems (e.g., Katz & Kahn, 1966; Thompson, 1967), organizational scholars have avoided inclusion of the customer or client in their thinking or their research (Bowen & Schneider, 1988). In a quotation that still applies today, Danet (1981) noted that

> Organization theorists have viewed organizations from the top looking down or from the inside looking around. The first of the organization theorists' perspectives has emphasized the problems of management, and the second has been directed at such issues as workers' satisfaction and role behavior. Thus, organization theorists have hardly mentioned clients at all. (p. 382)

Given the role that HRM/OB might play in increasing our understanding of service delivery and service quality, it is baffling how little emphasis service delivery receives from HRM/OB researchers and practitioners. Our conclusion is that HRM/OB researchers focus more on internal processes than they do on external consequences, and they focus more on individual-level accomplishments than they do on organizational consequences. The focus of these fields on internal, individual processes (e.g., motivation, attitudes, ability, personality, performance appraisal) has unfortunately led them to ignore the connections between internal organizational processes and externally relevant consequences and accomplishments (Dobbins, Cardy, & Carson, 1991).

Integrated Approaches From Services Management

In this section, we will explore ways in which we can integrate the seemingly different disciplines of marketing, OM, and HRM/OB to develop a more holistic view of organizations that deliver service to customers.

Basically, the different functions of an organization must all operate together under a shared service logic if customers are to perceive high service quality and if they are to be satisfied (Kingman-Brundage, George, & Bowen, 1999). By "logic," we are referring to the implicit and explicit principles that drive organizational performance.

Creating a shared service logic can be difficult if different functions within an organization have different goals. Marketing may focus on raising sales as high as possible, while the OM department may focus on efficiency. In order to deliver quality service to customers, however, these functions must consider both of these goals as subordinate to the higher-order principle of a service logic and adjust accordingly. Marketing may be constrained to raise sales only to a specified level—one that can be supported with the quality of service the organization wants to deliver. OM may have to compromise efficiency to some extent for the delivery of individualized service to customers—again at a level consistent with the quality of service the organization wants to deliver. In turn, HRM policies and practices can help to create this service logic and bind departments with different goals together.

One might think of this integrated perspective toward service management as a process of "de-siloing": We are attempting to get away from disciplinary silos and to focus on quality and the customer from a number of vantage points simultaneously. We do this for two reasons. First, there is a practical driver in that customers experience all of these facets of organizations simultaneously or at least as an integrated sequence. Second, there is potential for identifying interesting theoretical and research opportunities for the future.

Of course, we already have several hints for the potential of "de-siloing" to shed important and interesting light on issues of interest. For example, consider the excellent article by Drew and Bolton (1995) about using customer, employee, and OM procedural data to triangulate on customer satisfaction. While they show the relationships between employee and customer data, and between operational measures and customer data, they do not address the relationships between operational data and employee data. Including this link would illustrate effects for all three combinations of the data collected, but our examination of the research literature indicates that this is rarely, if ever, done.

Indeed, as we thought through the possibilities for combining these different sources of data related to service quality, we realized that we actually found little theory or empirical research on the degree to which OM processes link to employee experiences. For example, what are the consequences to employees of working in high-customer-contact organizations? In one of the few studies on this topic, Weatherly and Tansik (1993) found that the strategies that employees use to deal with customers (e.g., effort, negotiating, preempting, avoiding) have implications for their levels of job satisfaction and role stress. More specifically, Weatherly and Tansik found that effort as a strategy yields higher levels of job satisfaction, and negotiating as a strategy yields increased levels of role ambiguity and role conflict. Other work shows that employees who experience stress as service providers have customers with lower levels of reported service quality (Parkington & Schneider, 1979).

The bottom line here is that crossing the three disciplines in the same study might yield increased insight into the role of each in understanding the other. Let us see what has been happening in the way of such integrated frameworks for pushing along the integrated study of service quality.

The Service Profit Chain

Heskett, Sasser, and Schlesinger (1997) summarized many years of theory and research in their book on *The Service Profit Chain*. (See Hallowell and Schlesinger [2000] for an up-to-date review of the model.) The basic ideas behind the service profit chain are summarized in Figure 5.1.

Figure 5.1 shows that when the internal organization is designed in ways that promote employee capability (through selection and development), satisfaction (through job design, rewards, and recognition), productivity (through tools and resources), and service quality (through all of the above), then a likely consequence is employee loyalty. Having employees who are loyal and satisfied helps to create service value for customers—but this does not happen without input from operations with regard to quality and productivity improvements (e.g., reengineering). This latter element, we will see, is often ignored in research that tests the tenets of the service profit chain. In any case, an outcome of improved service values is customer satisfaction and loyalty, which are in turn proposed to yield improved revenue growth and profitability.

144

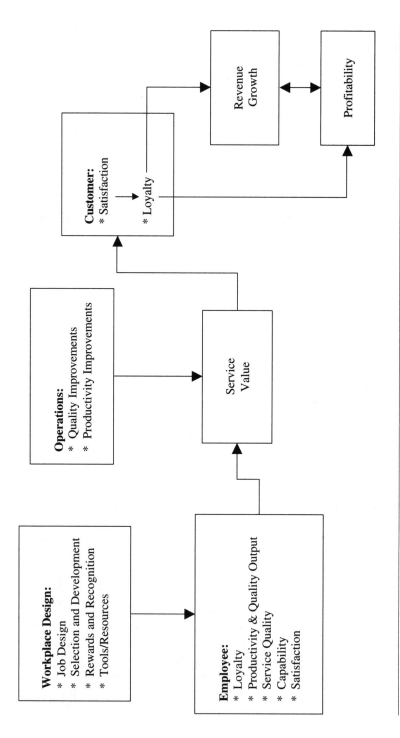

Figure 5.1   The Service Profit Chain

SOURCE: Reprinted by permission of *Harvard Business Review.* From "Putting the service profit chain to work" by Heskett et al., March/April 1994. Copyright © 1994 by the Harvard Business School Publishing Corporation; all rights reserved.

Heskett, Sasser, and Schlesinger (1997) marshal a large amount of anecdotal and hard research evidence to support the various links shown in Figure 5.1, including the linkage of operations and employee contributions to service value and customer satisfaction and loyalty. Take their Southwest Airlines example as an instance of how important all facets of the service profit chain model are for revenues and profits. What Heskett et al. (1997) show is that a combination of workplace and job design accompanied by careful selection and development yield a loyal, capable work force. Add this to the finding that careful attention to the operational issues concerning airplane maintenance timing and efficiency in loading/unloading of baggage and passengers (at almost double the efficiency of any other airline) results in lower costs per passenger, less expensive tickets, and high levels of service quality. Voilà! We see satisfied and loyal customers as well as improved revenues and profits.

Our point here is that it is not just happy employees that do the trick. Schneider and Bowen (1995) called the simplistic idea that it is all in the people "the human resources trap." What Heskett et al. (1997) show is that it is the combination of people or employee issues with attention to operational detail that produce customer satisfaction and loyalty. Yet their approach is frequently summarized with the sound bite of the "satisfaction mirror," suggesting that satisfied employees yield satisfied customers—and that if one understands this simplistic silver bullet, then everything good follows. It just ain't so!

Let us look in detail at a few pieces of research to see how the model has been tested. Loveman (1998) presented a relatively complete test of his version of the service profit chain, presented in Figure 5.2. (We say "his version," because no data were collected with regard to the operational issues in the middle of Figure 5.1.) He tested his model on 450 bank branches, using data collected in two time periods. All of his analyses were at the branch level of analysis, and he had data on the following variables: profitability (revenue per full-time equivalent employee [FTE] per household), customer loyalty (account retention), customer satisfaction (rankings and ratings provided by customers), employee loyalty (both actual tenure and survey data on commitment), employee satisfaction (survey data), and internal service quality (as rated by employees—not dissimilar from the internal service quality scale used by Schneider, White, & Paul, 1998).[1]

Using bivariate correlations of adjacent variables, Loveman (1998) reported some support for his model. Note that he did not have access to any data on external service quality, so the adjacent variables in the

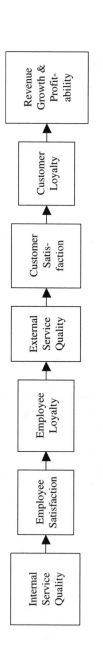

Figure 5.2   Loveman's (1998) Service Profit Chain

SOURCE: From Loveman, G. W. (1998) "Employee satisfaction, customer loyalty, and financial performance: An empirical examination of the service profit chain in retail banking," in *Journal of Service Research, 1,* pp. 18-31. Reprinted with permission from Sage Publications, Inc.

middle of the model concern employee loyalty and customer satisfaction. Here, while a significant relationship was observed between actual employee tenure and customer satisfaction, there was no significant relationship between survey data on employee loyalty and customer satisfaction. In addition, Loveman tested for the satisfaction mirror (i.e., employee satisfaction–to–customer satisfaction relationship) and found no significant relationship when exploring customer satisfaction with the *branch*. What did emerge, however, was a significant relationship between employee satisfaction and customer satisfaction with the *bank*—indexed at the branch level of analysis. (As mentioned in Note 1, sometimes banks have branches because of what they do for the bank as a whole rather than for branch profitability reasons, and Loveman's data reveal how this might be true.)

We can summarize Loveman's (1998) work as follows: There is a relationship at the branch level of analysis between some internal organizational employee issues and customer satisfaction and loyalty. Unmeasured in his work were the employee issues (e.g., workplace and job design, selection and development, rewards and recognition,), and the operational procedure issues (product quality and production improvements) shown on the left and in the middle of Figure 5.1. The former are reminiscent of the climate research done by Schneider and his colleagues (e.g., Schneider et al., 1998) and others (e.g., Rogg, Schmidt, Shull, & Schmitt, 2001), who show a relationship between employee experiences of these internal organizational design issues focused on service quality and customer satisfaction. The latter finding appears, as noted in Chapter 4, to be quite robust, so that we can assume it will exist in many setting and studies.

Of course, such a statement is always an overstatement. Researchers learn early that they can never assume a relationship will always emerge. With regard to the satisfaction mirror idea, for example, Silvestro and Cross (2000) empirically tested the service profit chain in grocery retail stores in the United Kingdom. They found support for many of the hypothesized linkages, but not for the employee satisfaction or employee loyalty and customer satisfaction linkage. Silvestro and Cross viewed the satisfaction mirror as a central construct in the work of Heskett et al. (1997)—and it is an important concept—but Figure 5.1 clearly shows that the connections are mediated by what else the organization does to create value. What makes the results discovered by Silvestro and Cross perhaps quite stimulating is their finding of a significant *negative* relationship between employee and customer satisfaction. This finding recalls results discussed earlier by Sutton and Rafaeli (1988), wherein "quick service" retail food stores with the most satisfied customers were the least profitable. We desperately need some more contingency thinking to help explain these anomalies— something we will attempt later in the chapter.

The relationships among customer satisfaction, customer loyalty, and profitability also appear to be quite robust. For example, Hallowell (1996) studied 59 divisions of a retail bank and revealed significant relationships, as one would hypothesize from the service profit chain. Hallowell studied divisions of the bank rather than branches for several reasons. First, the bank considered the division as the strategic business unit, and managers of the divisions were held accountable for those units. Second, and very important for this kind of work, division profitability data were available in this study. The salience of Hallowell's use of the division as the unit of analysis is that it means that Chapter 5 of the current book reviews research in retail banks at the individual customer level of analysis (Yoon, Beatty, & Suh, 2001), the branch level (Loveman, 1998), and the division level (Hallowell, 1996). It is not every day that one gets to read about research carried out at such different levels of analysis, all of which report similar patterns of relationships.[2]

Summary. The service profit chain represents an essential breakthrough to the future of the integrated study of service quality. What is unique about the model is that it looks at service organizations as composed of people and processes internally and at the implications of those people and processes for the external customer and firm revenues and profitability. Outsiders to the world of research on service quality would say to themselves, "Well, that certainly makes sense." Insiders know that such integrative models across academic silos are rarely done. They are rare not only because of the academic silos issue, but also because of the sometimes overwhelming data demands they present for empirical testing. In their original book on the topic, Heskett et al. (1997) had to piece together different pieces of research looking at two or three variables at a time to provide tests for the various pieces of the model. The few tests available of the entire framework have largely supported it, although we note that most tests fail to consider the importance of the middle of the model concerning OM issues, such as total quality management (TQM) and productivity improvements (reengineering; see Lawler, Mohrman, & Ledford, 1998). We would further suggest that work on customer contact, yield management, estimates of return on quality, and so forth, as discussed in Chapter 3, need much more emphasis in our understanding of service quality and customer satisfaction. We will turn to this issue later, after we review the writings of Lovelock (2000, 2001) on integrating across marketing, OM, and HRM/OB.

Lovelock's Vantage on Integration for Understanding Service Quality

Lovelock (2000, 2001) has been the most persistent advocate for integrated perspectives for gaining insight into service quality, although he is certainly not the only one (see, for example, Grönroos, 1990; Looy, Dierdonck, & Gemmel, 1998). Lovelock's 2001 book is the most complete text detailing the ways in which different disciplines contribute simultaneously to an understanding of service quality in organizations.

Lovelock's treatment of the issues is quite practical in that his focus is on continuously enhancing the service quality that organizations deliver. That is, his focus is on how to make service organizations more effective. Therefore, his presentation is quite prescriptive, while simultaneously being grounded in theory and data. Kurt Lewin (1951), one of the fathers of modern social and industrial and organizational (I-O) psychology, said that "there is nothing so practical as a good theory" (p. 169). When one reads Lovelock, one begins to believe there is nothing so theoretical as good practice!

One of the things we like the most about Lovelock's prescriptive stance is that it suggests the kind of contingency perspectives we believe are the next frontier for research in service quality. His proposals are intuitively appealing—but so few of them have received research attention![3] For example, Lovelock (2000) asks the following contingency and strategic question: "How should marketing relate to operations and human resources in those service environments where production and consumption take place simultaneously?" (p. 424). The contingency issue is the simultaneity of production and consumption (meaning close customer contact). The question, of course, can be turned around as follows: *What should the HRM strategy look like when there is simultaneous production and consumption in the delivery of service to customers?* These questions suggest that, at a minimum, one needs to conceptualize the degree to which there is simultaneous production and consumption when thinking about marketing and HRM. Lovelock's

Table 5.1   What Marketing Should Do When There Is Simultaneous Production
                   and Consumption of Services

---

1. Evaluate and select the market segment to serve;

2. Research consumer needs and preferences within each segment;

3. Monitor competitive offerings, identifying their principal characteristics, their quality levels, and the strategies used to bring them to market;

4. Design the core product, tailor its characteristics to the needs of the chosen market segments, and ensure that they match or exceed those of competitive offerings;

5. Select and establish service levels for supplementary elements needed to enhance the value and appeal of the core product or to facilitate its purchase and use;

6. Participate in designing the entire service process to ensure that it is "user friendly" and reflects customer needs and preferences;

7. Set prices that reflect costs, competitive strategies, and consumer sensitivity to different price levels;

8. Tailor location and scheduling of service availability to customer needs and preferences;

9. Develop communication strategies, using appropriate media to transmit messages informing prospective customers about the service and promoting its advantage;

10. Develop performance standards for establishing and measuring service quality levels;

11. Create programs for rewarding and reinforcing customer loyalty; and

12. Conduct research to evaluate customer satisfaction following service delivery and identify any aspects requiring changes or improvements.

SOURCE: From Lovelock, C. (2000). "Functional integration in service: Understanding the links between marketing, operations, and human resources." In T. A. Swartz & D. Iacobucci (Eds.), *Handbook of services marketing and management.* Used with permission from Sage Publications, Inc.

(2000) answer is summarized in Table 5.1. This looks like a nice program of research to us!

You can see that Lovelock's (2000) approach to what marketing can do is to (a) pay attention to what we know from marketing, (b) pay attention to what we know from HRM/OB, and (c) pay attention to what we know from OM. Why is this so rarely done in practice? Lovelock (2000) addresses the issue in the following way:

> As service firms place more emphasis on marketing, there is increased potential for conflict among the three functions, especially between marketing and operations. Marketing managers are likely to see the operations perspective as narrow and one-sided. Similarly they may get frustrated by employee resistance to change

or labor agreements that constrain the firm's ability to introduce new services and innovative delivery systems. How comfortably can the three functions coexist in service businesses, and how are their relative roles perceived? (p. 427)

The metalevel conceptual issues Lovelock raises here require attention. What are the boundary conditions under which the three functions can be coordinated such that the result is superior performance of the firm? What role does the management of employees play in this coordination effort? For which kinds of services and market segments is coordination more or less important? For example, is coordination across functions as important in a cafeteria environment (a cost orientation) as it is in a white linen tablecloth environment (a revenue orientation)? Or, consider a call center environment, where credit card customers call in to speak with customer service representatives, versus the same situation in a private bank, where clients call in to request services. In which environment will marketing predominate, in which will operations predominate, and what are the implications for the different environments for HRM strategy? In some early work, Schneider and his colleagues (Schneider, Parkington, & Buxton, 1980) had an item in the employee survey that read as follows: "We are well prepared by marketing for the introduction of new products and services." Bank branches in which employees reported this was true were rated by customers as delivering superior quality service.

Lovelock (2000, p. 429) does an excellent job of summarizing the coordination and contingency issues with which the three functions in service firms must grapple. By doing so, he outlines for potential scholars and researchers some of the issues requiring our attention.

1. *The marketing imperative.* The firm will target specific types of customers whom it is well equipped to serve, then create ongoing relationships with them by delivering a carefully defined product package of "all actions and reactions" that they may desire to purchase.

2. *The operations imperative.* To create and deliver the specified service package to targeted customers, the firm will select those operational techniques that allow it to consistently meet customer-driven cost, schedule, and quality goals, and also enable the business to reduce its costs through continuing improvements in productivity.

3. *The human resources imperative.* The firm will recruit, train, and motivate managers, supervisors, and employees who can work well together for a realistic compensation package to balance the twin goals

of customer satisfaction and operational effectiveness. People will want to stay with the firm and to enhance their own skills, because they value the working environment, appreciate the opportunities that it presents, and take pride in the services they help to create and deliver.

If Lovelock (2000) can manage to introduce HRM/OB into marketing, how can we introduce marketing and OM into HRM/OB?

Introducing Service Quality Into HRM/OB

We think the clearest path to introducing service quality into OB/HRM is through the vantage point of what has come to be called strategic human resources management (SHRM; see Delery & Doty, 1996). As we noted in some detail in Chapter 4, HRM practices, such as selection, training, and performance management, appear to be key ways organizations send the message to their employees that specific strategic imperatives are important. As we are interested here in the strategic importance of service quality, the question becomes one of identifying the ways by which the service quality message is sent via SHRM. In what follows, we first provide a bit of history on the topic of SHRM. Then we introduce our ideas about making SHRM specifically focused on service. So, similar to what we did with the generic concept of organizational climate and the strategic service climate, we here do the same thing with SHRM.

Strategic Human Resources Management (SHRM)

Broadly conceptualized, SHRM has been concerned with the contribution of HRM practices to organizational effectiveness. There has typically been an assumption that HRM practices are influential with regard to firm performance, but actual research—at the level of the firm—is relatively new. As Huselid (1995) put it,

> The belief that individual employee performance has implications for firm-level outcomes has been prevalent among academics and practitioners for many years. Interest in this area has recently intensified, however, as scholars have begun to argue that, collectively, a firm's employees can also provide a unique source of competitive advantage that is difficult for competitors to replicate. (p. 636)

The idea behind the use of the word *strategic* in SHRM has its roots in this notion of competitive advantage. Of particular importance to

Table 5.2   Sample Questions

- What is the proportion of the workforce whose job has been subjected to a formal job analysis?
- What proportion of non–entry level jobs have been filled from within in recent years?
- What is the proportion plans and/or gain sharing plans?
- What proportion of the workforce is administered an employment test prior to hiring?
- What proportion of the workforce receives formal performance appraisals?
- What is the proportion of the workforce whose performance appraisals are used to determine their compensation?

SOURCE: Adapted with permission from the Academy of Management. Copyright © 1995.

this vantage point has been the work emerging from the resource-based view of organizations. This view is that human capital is a potentially important firm resource that, when optimized, can provide a competitive advantage in the marketplace (Barney, 1991).

Huselid (1995; see also Huselid & Becker, 1996; Huselid, Jackson, & Schuler, 1997) presents an excellent example of the kinds of thinking and research that attempt to explore how and why HRM practices are actually reflected in firm performance. Huselid collected data on firm HRM practices from the HRM directors of 968 firms for whom he also had financial information on firm performance. HRM directors responded to items about the firm's personnel selection practices, performance appraisal systems, incentive and compensation systems, job design, grievance procedures, job analysis efforts, and so forth. Example questions appear above in Table 5.2.

It is clear from the examples shown in Table 5.2 that the focus of the issues assessed was the proportion of the employees in a firm subjected to various HRM practices. Note, however, that data were not collected on the sophistication of the practices (e.g., the validation of tests) or the quality of the outcomes of the processes (e.g., the talent level the job analyses revealed the firm requires). These comments are not meant as a criticism, as these issues were not the author's focus; they merely provide a backdrop to suggestions we will make later.

In any case, these survey data were studied at the firm level of analysis against firm-level turnover, productivity (logarithm of sales per employee), gross return on assets, and market value. Huselid's (1995) results revealed that different combinations of the HRM practices were reflected significantly (though modestly) in the four dependent

Table 5.3   Revised Sample Questions

- What is the proportion of the workforce whose job has been subjected to a formal job analysis *that focuses on the service requirements of the job?*
- What proportion of non–entry level jobs have been filled from within in recent years *by explicitly focusing on the service competencies of workers?*
- What is the proportion of the workforce who have access to company incentive plans, profit-sharing plans, and/or gain sharing plans *that depend for award on service performance excellence?*
- What proportion of the workforce is administered an employment test *that focuses on service competencies and personality* prior to hiring?
- What proportion of the workforce receives formal performance appraisals *that emphasize the facets of service delivery excellence?*
- What is the proportion of the workforce whose performance appraisals *of their service delivery performance* are used to determine their compensation?

variables of interest. For example, motivation systems (e.g., use of performance appraisals) were not related to turnover, but a focus on employee skills (e.g., use of tests, filling open jobs from within) was. Conversely, productivity was more strongly correlated with motivation systems than with a focus on employee skills.

Work in the area of SHRM conducted by Huselid and others (e.g., Delery & Doty, 1996; Hitt, Bierman, Shimizu, & Kochhar, 2001) tend to treat HRM practices in generic form. By this we mean that the HRM practices are viewed through the lens shown in Table 5.2: the relative use of performance appraisal, job analysis, testing, incentive systems, and so forth. Our view, in contrast, is that to be effectively strategic, HRM practices should focus on specific strategies of the firm—like service quality. To illustrate, compare the items presented above in Table 5.3 to those shown earlier in Table 5.2. In Table 5.3, we have added the notion of service quality as the strategic imperative.

Table 5.3 now reflects an assessment of the SHRM approach of an organization that has a strategic focus on service excellence. It is easy to add to the list of HRM practices that might be examined for the degree to which they focus on service excellence—training, for example, or socialization practices. Our major point is that SHRM approaches to firm effectiveness would do well to focus the HRM processes on strategic imperatives of interest—service quality in the present case.

What evidence is there that this specifically directed approach to SHRM practices can be more effective than simply doing generic HRM well? In this regard, an excellent study was accomplished by Youndt, Snell, Dean, and Lepak (1996). Youndt et al. approached their study by asking the following question: Do generically good HRM practices in combination with good contingent HRM practices (i.e., those that are contingent on particular organizational initiatives) provide superior understanding and prediction of organizational performance than generically good HRM practices alone? In Youndt et al.'s (1996) language, "According to the contingency approach to strategic human resources management (SHRM), . . . the impact of HR practices on firm performance is conditioned by an organization's strategic posture" (p. 841).[4]

Youndt et al. (1996) studied 97 firms in the primary metals industry and asked them about the degree to which they had most adopted as the path to success: a "cost strategy" (focus on controlling costs), a "quality strategy" (focus on product quality), or a "flexibility strategy" (focus on being agile and adaptive). Eighteen months later, they assessed performance of the organizations by resurveying the initial managers. Results revealed the following:

- There was a main effect for HRM practices on performance. In general, firms that had superior use of HRM practices performed significantly better than those that did not.
- There was a moderate effect of strategy on the relationship between HRM practices and organizational performance. More specifically, the more an organization adopted a "quality strategy," the stronger was the relationship between human capital HRM practices and performance. Conversely, in the "cost strategy" and the "flexibility strategy" categories, the interaction was with administrative approaches to HRM in the prediction of performance.

The message sent by Youndt et al.'s (1996) results is that HRM practices are most effective when they are aligned with the firm's overall competitive strategy (also see Bowen, 1996; Schuler, 1996).

In addition to the work just discussed, a second way that HRM practices can be aligned with the strategic outcome of interest is through the effects of HRM practices on strategically relevant mediating variables, such as climate. For example, Rogg et al. (2001) proposed that HRM practices are reflected in customer satisfaction to the degree that the HRM practices yield a strong customer service climate. They studied 351 small businesses (automotive franchise service dealerships) and showed that there is only a modest direct relationship between HRM practices and customer satisfaction, but that the HRM practices are strongly related to climate, which in turn is more strongly related to customer satisfaction. This work is reminiscent of the Schneider et al. (1998) paper, which showed that foundation issues[5] related to service climate, which in turn related to customer satisfaction. The important conclusion here is that the strongest correlate of customer satisfaction from an HRM perspective is the most proximal one—which is in turn most directly related to customer and service issues.

We have already presented the issue of alignment between HRM practices and strategic initiatives in some detail, but, before leaving the subject, we want to mention a very interesting conceptual paper on SHRM by Lepak and Snell (1999) because of its important implications for service organizations in particular. The authors propose that different HRM configurations in a company have implications for the value placed on human capital, the modes of employment adopted by the firm (e.g., contractual vs. developing), and then the nature of the relationship the employees have with the firm (e.g., transactional vs. symbiotic). Calling their framework one of "HR architecture," the arguments presented by Lepak and Snell might be extended to suggest that contractual workers will have a more transactional relationship with the firm and thus deliver lower levels of service quality to customers than employees who have a relationship that promotes their development and a more symbiotic relationship with the firm. To our knowledge, no research on these kinds of issues has been accomplished vis-à-vis customer satisfaction—an issue we will return to later. For now, we move to another approach to dealing with the management of organizational components—especially the human one—as correlates of organizational performance.

What might SHRM look like if it believed in OM and marketing, too? First, the issue of degree of customer contact would be introduced as a key contingency variable in how HRM is likely to be carried out. For example, if there is relatively low customer contact, perhaps less interpersonal competence and/or service orientation is required on the part of those hired and less time in training need be spent on such skills. The rule we would follow would be to ensure that job analyses always consider degree of customer contact as a key contingency issue in the design of selection, training, and performance management systems.

Also from OM, we are very persuaded by the materials discussed in Chapter 3 that OB/HRM conceptualizations and research have paid little attention to the impact of demand/capacity decisions and revenue management choices on employee experiences and/or the linkage of employee experiences to customer reports on service quality.

With regard to marketing, the key issue revealed in Lovelock (2001) concerns the segment of the market in which the service firm operates. This becomes key, because the nature of the expectations of different market segments is likely to affect the way the people in the organization relate to customers. While there is likely a relationship between degree of customer contact and market segment—with high customer contact being in higher priced and more customized service segments—the relationship will not be perfect. Thus again the nature of the kinds of employees sought, the way they are trained, the skills they are taught, and the key issues on which performance management processes must focus will vary as a function of market segment. To our knowledge, there is research on the implications of degree of customer contact neither for HRM practices nor for the differences associated with market segments.

In the last section of the chapter, we will return to some ways by which marketing and OM concepts and approaches can inform OB/HRM research.

The High Performance *Service* Organization

The premise underlying the generic concept of "the high-performance organization" is no different than the one underlying SHRM: The way organizations are managed has competitive advantage. Whereas SHRM has tended to focus on traditional HRM practices, such as those in Table 5.2, thinking and research on the high-performance organization (HPO) has focused on more OB issues, such as employee involvement tactics, TQM, and reengineering. This has been especially true at Lawler's Center for Effective Organization (CEO) at the University of Southern California, where studies are conducted on the HPO practices of the Fortune 1000. The CEO survey used to study the HPO practices is quite extensive in the coverage of the questions asked, focusing not only on practices but also on outcomes of those practices and the positive and negative experiences of associated with those practices. A number of practices are assessed in the HPO surveys, including (a) employee involvement issues, (b) TQM practices, and (c) reengineering practices.

- *Employee involvement:* The employee involvement issues assessed are a complex mélange, including work and job design, participation in decision making (empowerment), pay systems, the way organizational change is conceptualized and carried out, the use of teams, and a host of practices designed to improve the knowledge employees have to work in teams (e.g., information, training, and continuous learning practices).

• *TQM:* TQM (as discussed in Chapter 1) issues include the OM perspective on statistical quality control as well as an emphasis on teams and team decision making.

• *Reengineering:* Reengineering (as discussed in Chapter 1) is focused on information technology and the advantages of information technology with regard to cutting costs (through downsizing because of a need for fewer employees), increasing responsiveness (through the possibility of immediate responses, especially in the ordering departments of firms), and becoming closer to the customer (through intranet/Internet linkages to the customer). Many of the issues in Chapter 3 on OM are reviewed here.

By way of summary of the components of HPO and contrasts in them, see Table 5.4, developed by Lawler et al. (1998, p. 11).

The comparison of the approaches shown in Table 5.4 is reminiscent of early writings in OB by such historically important scholars as Argyris (1957) and McGregor (1960). In the case of Argyris, he argued that when management treats adult workers like children, their likely response is to behave like children. McGregor (1960) was equally clear in his presentation of Theory X and Theory Y. He noted that when managers have a Theory X philosophy about employees, they will behave in ways that focus on coercion, pay as the only reason for employment, lack of interest in doing challenging work and/or participation, and so forth. This stands in stark contrast to Theory Y, where managers think of employees as adults with broad interests and broad competencies who desire challenge and involvement.

A considerable benefit of the Lawler et al. (1998) HPO approach is that companies in the sample are asked to describe their use of practices associated with all three of the approaches shown in Table 5.4. By asking companies about all of these practices, it is possible to examine the relative effectiveness of organizations when they do one, two, or all three of the practices. For example, Lawler et al. found that

• Companies that use both employee involvement and TQM are more effective in the outcomes they achieve from TQM than those that only use TQM.

• It is unimportant whether a company introduces employee involvement or TQM first; it is important that they do both in an integrated fashion.

Table 5.4   Contrasts in Three Different Components of the HPO Approach to Managing Organizations

	Employee Involvement	Total Quality Management	Process Reengineering
Age	Young adult	Adolescent	Infant
Teams	Self-managing	Problem solving	Business process
Feedback	Business and unit performance	Customer feedback; quality levels	Process performance
Disciplinary Base	Social science	Quality engineering	Information technology
Implementation Process	Bottom-up	Top-down	Top-down
Preferred Work Design	Enriched	Simplified, standardized	Mixed
Unique Contributions	Group processes, motivational alignment, employee well-being	Quality emphasis, worker tools (e.g., statistical quality control)	Downsizing, process focus, technological change (especially information technology)

SOURCE: From Lawler, Mohrman, and Ledford (1998). *Strategies for High Performance Organizations.* This material is used with permission of John Wiley & Sons, Inc.

- Reengineering is associated with higher levels of firm effectiveness and performance when accompanied by TQM or employee involvement facets.
- Reengineering approaches combined with employee involvement approaches increase the effectiveness of the employee involvement approaches—especially with regard to organizational performance.
- The most effective organizations integrate employee involvement, TQM, and reengineering approaches.

The important point we want to make is that the coordinated use of these different but overlapping approaches to management produces organizational performance that exceeds the use of only one of them. Furthermore, two is better than one and three is better than two. What is not clear is the way these findings might emerge in a sample of organizations dominated by service employees or organizations. For example, Batt (1999) showed in a study of telephone company employees that employees who were working in self-managed teams outperformed those who were working in a TQM environment. Further analyses revealed that self-managed units outperformed TQM units, too. In this case, then, employee involvement (in the form of self-managed teams) significantly outperformed employees and units in a TQM effort. Additional analyses revealed that employee involvement combined with increased use of technology (reengineering) was superior to either alone. Again, the effect of combining approaches seems superior.

Where is the role of customer contact or the importance of market segmentation and customer loyalty in the research on HPOs? To our knowledge, these kinds of contingencies have not been introduced into the thinking on HPOs. We will return to this issue again later.

Summary

This section was about the focus on quality in OB/HRM. We explored two models from these disciplines, SHRM and HPOs, for hints about ways they could serve as foils for improving the service quality focus of OB/HRM. These two approaches suggested a number of alternative models that might be adopted if one had a service quality strategy.

From SHRM, we learned that we require more research like that of Youndt et al. (1996) to explore the roles of generic and contingent HRM practices in determining organizational effectiveness. To what degree are *targeted* HRM practices superior to generically positive HRM practices? Of course, as HRM practices are studied, it should not be forgotten that it is the *bundle* of HRM practices that has an impact, not just one or two of them. From the findings in the HPO literature, especially those of Lawler and his colleagues (e.g., Lawler et al., 1998) over the past decade or so, we learned that there are important consequences of taking a multipronged approach to organizational performance rather than focusing on only one or two approaches. That is, benefits in organizational performance are related to adopting TQM, employee involvement, and reengineering rather than trying to use one to accomplish all goals. One might even conclude that combining OB/HRM with OM can produce impressive results.

What is clear from the literature we examined is that customers and service quality are not seen as central to the management of organizations in the OB/HRM literatures. By way of summarizing this last chapter, we abstract from the works of Lovelock (2000; 2001) and Heskett et al. (1997) to develop an agenda for future research. Such research would be useful to tackle if the field of service quality is to continue to be both a source of inspiration for theory and research—as well as a field that is practically useful.

Conclusion: Future Research Agenda

In this section, we will identify some final issues—issues raised in the materials just presented and presented throughout the book—that require conceptual and empirical attention to move the field of service quality forward. We focus explicitly on the kind of work with which OB and HRM academics and practitioners should be concerned, because we in these areas have been the least involved in the exciting service revolution.

Research Questions

Question 1: Are firms more effective at satisfying customers when they de-silo?

An implicit if not explicit premise for our entire book, and a clear premise from Lovelock (2001), is that organizations that are (a) integrated cross-functionally and (b) aligned to provide customer satisfaction are (c) more effective organizations. This presumption makes an implicit assumption itself that conflict, tension, and disagreement between and across functions are bad for organizations.

The issue of integration in organizations is not new. Lawrence and Lorsch (1967), for example, noted that units within an organization simultaneously differ from one another and must cooperate with one another. In their research, they showed that the more ambiguous the environment or task for the firm, the less differentiated (more integrated) it should be for effective performance. This reflects the perspective that an integrated organization is more effective only under certain conditions (e.g., ambiguity of environment), rather than the universal perspective suggested by Lovelock (2001; and implicitly by us) of the value of integration. According to Donaldson's (2001) extensive review of the literature, there is very good empirical support for this contingent (organic) theory of organizations, suggesting to us that functional integration as a key to service quality will depend on (a) the need for innovation as a key to competitive effectiveness and (b) the necessity for tasks to be done interdependently. When the need for innovation is low and when task interdependence is low, the need for integration is also low—de-siloing may not be useful.

What is intriguing is that, to our knowledge, the research supporting the view that organizations should only be de-siloed conditionally was primarily, if not exclusively, accomplished in manufacturing organizations. Lawrence and Lorsch's (1967) organizations, as well as the organizations studied by Woodward (1965), as the start of this contingent/organic theory were all in the manufacturing sector. The degree to which organic theory also applies to service firms is not known and has received little attention, to our knowledge. For us, what is important about organic/contingent theory is that it proposes that universals are contingent—all is not the same given particular contingencies. In organic theory, the contingencies have to do with task attributes, the need for innovation, and the turbulence of the larger environment. For the study of service quality, especially within OB, we do not have similar contingency frameworks, with the exception of the work by Mills and his colleagues (Mills, 1986; Mills & Margulies, 1980; Mills & Moberg, 1982). In their work, the key contingency is the nature of the relationship with the customer as determined by the nature of the service being delivered. Some services are viewed as being dominated by the core service (e.g., the food at a restaurant), while others are dominated by the personal relationships developed with the client. In this perspective, the role of the service deliverer is conditional on the nature of the service—and the personal qualities of the service deliverer become more important to the service experience with, for example, "personal-interactive services" (Mills & Margulies, 1980). It is immediately obvious that this perspective on service types is reminiscent of Chase's (1978) customer-contact model, discussed in Chapter 3. There, we showed that degree of customer contact has important implications for the way the service is designed to be delivered and for the role that human service deliverers play in customer satisfaction. Thus, again, we see that there are contingencies on how organizations may be designed for service delivery as a function of the nature of the service to be delivered, especially the nature of the interaction with the customer.

We may conclude, building on organic theory and the perspectives of Mills and Chase (see Mills, Chase, & Margulies, 1983), that in nonturbulent environments and in environments where customer contact is low, organizations may prosper even with great differentiation among marketing, operations, and HRM. However, in environments where innovation in service is required to remain competitive and/or where customer contact is high, coordination across functions is more likely to be required to deliver quality service. Research on this hypothesis is required.

An interesting study in this regard is one reported by Verma (1997). Verma studied four different kinds of services (fast food, auto repair, retail sales, and legal services) to explore the challenges managers face in these very different kinds of service businesses. Using a classification scheme developed by Schmenner (1986) that focuses simultaneously on customer contact, customization (the uniqueness of the offering to customers), and labor intensity (the need for people for service delivery), Verma tested some of the management challenges in the Schmenner (1986) framework.[6] What he found was that type of service indeed has an impact on what managers perceive to be their greatest (and smallest) challenges. For example, Verma showed that, as services become increasingly customized or have increasing amounts of customer contact, scheduling service delivery and technological advances become greater challenges while attention to physical surroundings and scheduling of the workforce become lesser ones. These kinds of models, in which the implications of different attributes of services are studied, are clearly needed.

Question 2: Are firms more effective when they manage the HRM processes from a contingency perspective?

This second question is another form of the contingency question stated in Question 1. Here, the question concerns the degree to which the human resources (i.e., employees) of organizations are managed in accord with the targeted customers of the organization. That is, are universally good HRM practices equally appropriate across service types and market segments? In line with our thinking about Question 1, we think not. We believe that Lovelock (2000) would agree with us, but his point of view on this is not clear. For example, he notes that the marketing imperative is to ensure that "the firm will target specific types of customers whom it is well equipped to serve" (p. 429), but his HRM proposal is not specific with regard to the customers to be served. However, would we expect the HRM practices at McDonald's to be the same as the HRM practices at Chez Panisse? Of course not. The question is, How will they be different and how are we to think about those differences?

To be maximally strategic, our perspective is that HRM practices must be aligned with the segment that marketing strategically targets for the firm, just as Lovelock holds that operations must be aligned with the targeted market segment. Our proposal is reminiscent of our earlier review of what Davidow and Uttal (1989) called "focus or falter." Here, we add that firms that focus their HRM and operations procedures on their strategic market segment will deliver the highest levels of service quality *in their market segment* and have the highest levels of customer satisfaction *in their market segment* (Schneider, 1994). We highlight the phrase *in their market segment,* because we hypothesize that service firms need not try to achieve the highest possible scores on service quality or customer satisfaction surveys; rather, they should attempt to be in the lead in their market segment. One can have a cafeteria that receives lower scores on service quality than does the white-linen restaurant next door; what is important is to be the best cafeteria.

To our knowledge, there does not exist a contingency model for HRM issues in organizations. Thus, while contingent/organic theory exists for organizational design vis-à-vis differentiation and integration, no such model exists for the HRM foci required for firms operating in different environments—whether those environments differ in terms of turbulence, competitiveness, market segment, or degree of customer contact. A start in this direction has been taken by Mills (1986), and recent research by Batt (2000) is a good example of the ways service firms can match their employees and their HRM practices to the customer segment the firm is designed to reach. We pursue this idea in more detail in Question 3.

Question 3: How important are the personal attributes of service employees?

Customers are important because their satisfaction determines the future of the organization. OM is important because it provides the processes and procedures by which service is delivered and costs are kept down, thus providing for firm profitability. HRM/OB and I-O have been treated as important because they establish the climate in which service is delivered. Establishing and maintaining service climates (as well as other organizational climates) are seen to be management's responsibility: Management provides the training, the resources, the internal service, and so forth and also plans for, sets goals for, and facilitates service excellence. Then there are those who actually deliver the service.

Let us think contingently here. If (a) the service firm is in a stable environment with few competitors, (b) the service provided is low on customer contact, and (c) customers do not much participate in their own production, then the nature of the service employees may not be important. However, if the firm sees service quality as a competitive edge and the service is or can become high-contact, then the quality of the employees (and their training, support, etc.) become important. There is now good evidence that, in such environments, personality-type measures can be useful predictors of employee customer orientation. As noted earlier, Frei and McDaniel (1998) provided a meta-analysis of 41 validity studies using paper-and-pencil personality questionnaires targeted on service orientation.[7] The mean corrected validity coefficient across these studies was a robust $r = 0.50$. All of the studies included in this meta-analysis were validated against supervisory ratings of customer orientation.

From a construct vantage point, Frei and McDaniel (1998) segment their data by the personality dimensions in the Five Factor Model (FFM) of personality (see Hough & Schneider, 1996).[8] For service jobs, it appears that the dimensions called Agreeableness and Emotional Stability (sometimes called Neuroticism) are consistently the strongest correlates of the supervisory ratings (see Table 2 in Frei & McDaniel, 1998). Similar results are reported in Furnham and Coveney (1996), but Rogelberg, Barnes-Farrell, and Creamer (1999) did not find support for personality as a correlate of customer service behavior. They explain their lack of results as due to the sample they studied—customer service workers who dealt with customers via the telephone. This finding makes our point: We have little to no conceptual or empirical findings on potential contingencies affecting relationships between the personal attributes of employees and the service quality they deliver to customers. Perhaps personality is only considered, and therefore only validated, when customer contact is high such that the meta-analytic results reported will generalize only to such settings. Research is needed to explore this.

Question 4: Should OB/HRM focus more on service firm profits?

One of the reasons why service firms may pay so much attention to OM and marketing is because of a focus on the bottom line. In contrast, OB/HRM and allied fields seem to have our focus on internal processes and more human and humane employee outcomes. Even when we extend our vision to the external world, we typically focus on customer satisfaction—not on sales, costs, revenues, or profits. We have essentially left the issue of sales and revenues to others. Our impression is that this has not served us well in getting our theories and research accepted by management. In the final analysis, management is always more concerned with dollars than they are with anything else—at best, they are concerned with tomorrow's dollars.

To help address this gap, Schneider and his colleagues (Schneider, Ehrhart, Mayer, & Saltz, 2002) have begun doing some research that focuses on dollars, too. That is, like the service profit chain, which runs from employee issues through operational issues to customer outcomes and firm revenues and profits, Schneider et al. have started to conceptualize the service organization as a process organization, one that simultaneously includes employee attributes and behavior, the consequences of those behaviors for internal organizational atmosphere, and the consequences of that atmosphere for customer satisfaction and then sales. A working framework for this approach is shown in Figure 5.3.

The "department" mentioned in Figure 5.3 refers to the departments in supermarkets (e.g., produce, meat, dairy), the context in which the research to date has been accomplished. This framework views the personality of the leader to be an important starting point for the service behaviors required by him or her to create a service climate. In turn, it is assumed that a service climate is one that promotes behaviors towards customers that will produce high-quality customer experiences and customer satisfaction. These customer experiences are likely tied fairly directly to sales and thus to revenues and profits. There is some preliminary evidence in support of the model (Schneider et al., 2002).

The model showed the following:

1. Individual differences in department manager personality were correlated significantly with the ratings department employees made of the service leadership behavior of the department manager.

2. In turn, these ratings of service leadership were significantly related to reports of service climate and organizational citizenship behavior (OCB) (controlling for same-source bias by randomly splitting employees in each department into two groups).

3. Both OCB and service climate independently correlated with customer satisfaction (though OCB was the stronger correlate).

4. Customer satisfaction, in turn, correlated significantly with revenues.

Although the model did not explicitly consider OM issues, the service climate measure used with employees contained two items of the sort that would be of interest to OM researchers: (1) *We have sufficient staff in my department to deliver quality service* and (2) *Employees in my department are given sufficient work hours for us to deliver quality service.* These are the kinds of issues that Verma (1997) would refer to as "labor intensity" and that are typically not considered in OB and HRM

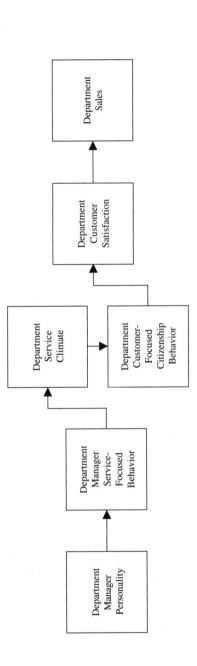

Figure 5.3 A Framework for Research That Simultaneously Considers Employee Issues, Organizational Issues, Customer Satisfaction, and Sales (Schneider et al., 2002)

research, where the focus is on the quality of people rather than the numbers. To make a long story short, in departments where employees report they have higher levels of sufficient staff and sufficient hours (no one ever reports they have enough; the issue is how high a department is compared to other departments), customers report higher levels of customer satisfaction and revenues are therefore higher. Analyses of the return on quality (Rust et al., 1996) associated with enhanced levels of staff and hours are still to be done.

Question 5: Is their a link between SERVQUAL dimensions and service climate dimensions? And what role does OM play?
   In Chapter 2, we described the development of SERVQUAL and other similar measures of service quality. The importance of these measures over measures of customer satisfaction resided in the fact that service quality facets are perceptions of events and reports of experiences, whereas customer satisfaction measures tend to be more purely affective reactions to events and experiences. With more descriptive information, the probability is increased that actions can be taken to ameliorate deficiencies.
   In Chapter 4, we described the development of service climate measures and, again, the focus was on descriptions of events—and also practices—under the same logic as that presented for SERVQUAL. In addition, recall that almost nothing in Chapter 4 referred to employee satisfaction; the focus was always on employee reports of events, practices, and procedures vis-à-vis service quality or what we called *foundation issues* on which a service climate might be created and maintained.
   In Chapter 4, we also showed that overall service quality reports from customers and overall service climate reports from employees were consistently and significantly linked across a wide variety of studies (Schneider, Bowen, Ehrhart, & Holcombe, 2000). However, those linkage studies did not proceed dimension by dimension. Rather, they focus on global service climate and global service quality.
   It would appear to be both practically useful and conceptually interesting to study dimension-by-dimension relationships from customer reports of service quality and employee reports of service climate. Conceptualize a matrix, then, defined by SERVQUAL dimensions for the rows and service climate dimensions for the columns. Data would then be collected and linkages run, and the matrix would be filled with correlation coefficients indicating where the strongest (and weakest) links might be. Such data could then be used as a diagnostic tool

whereby the strongest relationships would indicate tight links between climate dimensions and quality dimensions. Tight relationships would indicate that firms desiring to improve quality reports from customers would focus their efforts on improving the appropriate climate dimensions as experienced by employees.

We have learned something else in the book: OM issues matter, too. So, it becomes clear in this exercise, as the service profit chain (see Figure 5.1) and Lovelock's perspective (see Table 5.4) would indicate, that OM issues are missing from the linkages that would characterize the matrix described above. For example, one possibility is that degree of customer contact might moderate relationships in the matrix. Another possibility is that demand-capacity tradeoff decisions at different units would also moderate relationships in the matrix and/or serve as main effects. At the time we were completing this book, airlines were going through horrific revenue losses and both the number of flights were being cut and the proportion of cabin attendants per flying passenger were being reduced. Of course, these actions were taken based on revenue management issues, as discussed in Chapter 3.

The interesting question is whether and/or how such actions would affect (a) employee reports on various service climate dimensions, (b) customer reports on various service quality dimensions, and (c) the relationships among the climate and quality dimensions. Our hypothesis is that there would be mean differences in climate and quality data, but the relationships in the matrix would remain the same *if the changes were uniform across airlines.* If some airlines decrease the number of flights less than others (e.g., Southwest, at the time, was decreasing the number of flights less than United) and if some airlines (or flights within airlines) were decreasing cabin attendants proportionately less than other airlines (or flights), then these differences in changes become potential moderators of the relationships in the matrix.

More specifically, our hypothesis is that the more an airline cuts flights and cabin attendants, the stronger the relationship becomes between customer reports and employee experiences. The logic here is that the more an event is mutually experienced by employees and customers, the more they will share in their reports. Note that similar logic reveals the hypothesis that, in high-customer-contact facilities or services, there will be a stronger relationship between employee experiences and customer experiences—the higher the level of interaction between server and served, the stronger the relationships will be in the matrix.

Question 6: How about customer participation?

To our minds, the most interesting OM variable that might potentially serve as a key issue for linking marketing, HRM/OB, and OM concerns customer participation in production. Customer participation is not the same as customer contact. While the former has to do with interactions to accomplish service production and delivery, the latter has to do with mere presence. For example, attending a symphony concert entails mere presence for the service act. One might ask the interesting question: How different would the audience member perceptions of the service experience be if he or she participated in the concert? One might ask a perhaps more unusual question: How different would the experience for orchestra members be if members of the *audience* participated in the concert? We can generalize this question to any service production and delivery: How different are employee experiences and customer experiences when customers participate in production?

OM, of course, has done the most work conceptualizing the issue of customer participation, because it tends to increase heterogeneity in service production and delivery.[9] However, to our knowledge, the growing role that customer participation is playing in service work has not received much research attention. What are the long-term consequences of such participation as "self" check-in at the airlines, "self" diagnosis of computer problems via telephone contacts with service personnel, and so forth? Of course, in reality, all of these "self" activities require assistance from the service-delivering employee. So, if this growing participation were studied, OM might be inclined to keep it due to savings in labor costs, and marketing might like it because it breeds commitment and loyalty. However, HRM/OB might find it leads to increased employee stress and possible dissatisfaction, absenteeism, and turnover among employees.

The cautionary point here is that all good things will not necessarily follow from integration of the OM, marketing, and HRM/OB perspectives. That is, by each of the three fields attempting to optimize on what it does best (customer satisfaction, revenues, employee turnover), negative consequences may follow for another area. We are reminded here of an item in one of Schneider et al.'s (1980) early branch bank climate surveys: "We are well-prepared by Marketing for the introduction of new products and services" (p. 258). Positive responses to this item were associated with lower levels of employee stress. Thus, in order to lower employee stress, marketing had to take time away from advertising products and services to customers to prepare branch employees on these new products and services. So, compromises may have to be made to allow optimization of the *combined* outcome—attracting customers and keeping employee stress down—even though no one outcome is optimized.

Theory and research like the last two hypothetical integrations of OM, marketing, and HRM/OB presented in Questions 5 and 6 would be very useful and very interesting. We hope this brief volume has stimulated such thinking and will result in such research!

Notes

1. Loveman (1998) notes many of the problems inherent in doing this kind of research, perhaps the biggest being the need to adjust the model to the data available and the need to tailor operationalizations of variables to make them appropriate for the sample. The former issue in his work concerned the definition of profitability—a definition that has been a difficult issue for bank branches for a long time. Thus some branches are useful because they provide for overall bank profitability, not because they are individually profitable. This happens when a few important customers have access to a branch that has few other customers, for example. The latter issue—tailoring the data collected to the research site—is always a problem, because some issues are more or less relevant in some firms than in others. For example, Rucci, Kim, and Quinn (1998) reported on results of the application of the service profit chain at Sears and used very different indicators than did Loveman, making comparability of results at least a challenge.

2. Schneider has been asked why he and so many other linkage researchers study banks. His reply is that, when Willie Sutton was asked why he holds up so many banks, his reply was, "That's where all the money is."

3. Lovelock's penchant for contingency approaches should come as no surprise. The reader will recall from Chapter 3 that his different ways of conceptualizing services were essentially contingency approaches—the idea was to classify services so that one would gain marketing insights. And don't forget that these are models he developed in the early 1980s (Lovelock, 1983)!

4. Wright, Smart, and McMahan (1995), for example, have shown that basketball teams that acquired players who fit the strategy of the coach were more effective than teams that paid less attention to the coaching strategy in acquiring players.

5. The term *foundation issues* captured the concept of support provided by the organization to employees for doing their jobs.

6. In fact, Verma (1997) provides a very nice review of prior schemes for classifying services and the management challenges they suggest.

7. The personality questionnaire used for most of these reported studies was the one based on the Hogan Personality Inventory (HPI; Hogan & Hogan, 1995) and the measure within the HPI originally developed by Hogan, Hogan, and Busch (1984). Other results in the paper were based on a measure of Customer Relations developed by London House (1994).

8. The five dimensions of the FFM are Openness to Experience, Conscientiousness, Extraversion, Emotional Stability/Neuroticism, and Agreeableness. The use of measures of the FFM has proven quite useful for a variety of purposes, usually revealing that Conscientiousness most reliably predicts job performance.

9. Recall our earlier discussion that heterogeneity is raised to a whole new level when different customers participate in production instead of just appearing for the service act. While some customers will have the talent and/or desire to participate, others will have neither (Bateson, 1983; Lengnick-Hall, 1996; Schneider & Bowen, 1995).

References

Argyris, C. (1957). *Personality and organization.* New York: Harper.

Armstrong, G., & Kotler, P. (2003). *Marketing: An introduction* (6th ed.). Englewood Cliffs, NJ: Prentice Hall.

Barney, J. (1991). Firm resources and sustained competitive advantage. *Journal of Management, 17,* 99–120.

Bateson, J. E. G. (1983). The self-service customer—empirical findings. In L. Berry, G. L. Shostack, & G. D. Upah (Eds.), *Emerging perspectives in services marketing* (pp. 50-53). Chicago: American Marketing Association.

Batt, R. (1999). Work organization, technology, and performance in customer service and sales. *Industrial and Labor Relations Review, 52,* 539–564.

Batt, R. (2000). Strategic segmentation in front-line services: Matching customers, employees and human resource systems. *International Journal of Human Resource Management, 11,* 540–561.

Bowen, D. E. (1996). Market-focused HRM in service organizations: Satisfying internal and external customers. *Journal of Market-Focused Management, 1,* 31–48.

Bowen, D. E., & Schneider, B. (1988). Services marketing and management: Implications for organizational behavior. In B. M. Staw & L. L. Cummings (Eds.), *Research in organizational behavior* (Vol. 10, pp. 43–80). Greenwich, CT: JAI.

Chase, R. B. (1978). Where does the customer fit in a service operation? *Harvard Business Review, 56,* 137–142.

Chase, R. B., Aquilano, N. J., & Jacobs, E. R. (1998). *Production and operations management: Manufacturing and services* (8th ed.). San Francisco: Irwin/McGraw-Hill.

Danet, B. (1981). Client-organization relationships. In P. C. Nystrom & W. H. Starbuck (Eds.), *Handbook of organizational design* (Vol. 2, pp. 382–428). Oxford, England: Oxford University Press.

Davidow, W. H., & Uttal, B. (1989). Service companies: Focus or falter. *Harvard Business Review, 69,* 77–85.

Delery, J. E., & Doty, D. H. (1996). Modes of theorizing in strategic human resource management: Tests of universalistic, contingency, and configural performance predictions. *Academy of Management Journal, 39,* 802–835.

Dobbins, G. H., Cardy, R. L., & Carson, K. P. (1991). Examining fundamental assumption: A contrast of person and system approaches to human resource management. In K. M. Rowland & G. R. Ferris (Eds.), *Research in personnel and human resources management* (Vol. 9, pp. 1–38). Greenwich, CT: JAI.

Donaldson, L. (2001). *The contingency theory of organizations.* Thousand Oaks, CA: Sage.

Drew, J. H., & Bolton, R. N. (1995). Linking customer intelligence to service operations: Exploiting the connection at GTE. In T. A. Schwartz, D. E. Bowen, & S. W. Brown (Eds.), *Advances in services marketing and management* (Vol. 4., pp. 119–140). Greenwich, CT: JAI.

Fitzimmons, J. A., & Fitzimmons, M. J. (1994). *Service management for competitive advantage.* New York: McGraw-Hill.

Frei, R. L., & McDaniel, M. A. (1998). Validity of customer service measures in personnel selection: A review of criterion and construct evidence. *Human Performance, 11*(1), 1–27.

Furnham, A., & Coveney, R. (1996). Personality and customer service. *Psychological Reports, 79,* 675–681.

Grönroos, C. (1990). *Service management and marketing: Managing the moments of truth in service competition.* Lexington, MA: Lexington Books.

Hallowell, R. (1996). The relationships of customer satisfaction, customer loyalty, and profitability: An empirical study. *International Journal of Service Industry Management, 7,* 27–42.

Hallowell, R., & Schlesinger, L. A. (2000). The service profit chain: Intellectual roots, current realities, and future prospects. In T. A. Swartz & D. Iacobucci (Eds.), *Handbook of services marketing and management* (pp. 203–221). Thousand Oaks, CA: Sage.

Heskett, J. L., Sasser, W. E., Jr., & Schlesinger, L. A. (1997). *The service profit chain: How leading companies link profit and growth to loyalty, satisfaction, and value.* New York: Free Press.

Hitt, M. A., Bierman, L., Shimizu, K., & Kochhar, R. (2001). Direct and moderating effects of human capital on strategy and performance in professional service firms: A resource-based perspective. *Academy of Management Journal, 44,* 13–28.

Hogan, J., & Hogan, R. (1995). *Hogan personality inventory manual* (2nd ed.). Tulsa, OK: Hogan Assessment Systems.

Hogan, J., Hogan, R., & Busch, C. (1984). How to measure service orientation. *Journal of Applied Psychology, 69,* 167–173.

Hough, L. M., & Schneider, R. J. (1996). Personality traits, taxonomies, and applications in organizations. In K. R. Murphy (Ed.), *Individual differences and behavior in organizations* (pp. 31–88). San Francisco: Jossey-Bass.

Huselid, M. A. (1995). The impact of human resource management practices on turnover, productivity, and corporate financial performance. *Academy of Management Journal, 38,* 635–672.

Huselid, M. A., & Becker, B. E. (1996). Methodological issues in cross-sectional and panel estimates of the human resource-firm performance link. *Industrial Relations, 35,* 400–422.

Huselid, M. A., Jackson, S. E., & Schuler, R. S. (1997). Technical and strategic human resource management effectiveness as determinants of firm performance. *Academy of Management Journal, 40,* 171–188.

Katz, D., & Kahn, R. (1966). *The social psychology of organizations.* New York: John Wiley.

Kerin, R. A., Berkowitz, E. N., Hartley, S. W., & Rudelius, W. (2002). *Marketing* (7th ed.). New York: McGraw-Hill/Irwin.

Kingman-Brundage, J., George, W., & Bowen, D. E. (1999). Service logic: Achieving service system integration. *International Journal of Service Industry Management, 6*(4), 20–39.

Krajewski, L. J., & Ritzman, L. P. (2002). *Operations management: Strategy and analysis* (6th ed.). Upper Saddle River, NJ: Prentice Hall.

Lawler, E. E., III, Mohrman, S. A., & Ledford, G. E., Jr. (1998). *Strategies for high performance organizations: Employee involvement, TQM, and reengineering programs in Fortune 1000 corporations.* San Francisco: Jossey-Bass.

Lawrence, P. K., & Lorsch, J. W. (1967). *Organization and environment: Managing differentiation and integration.* Cambridge, MA: Harvard University, Graduate School of Business Administration, Division of Research.

Lengnick-Hall, C. A. (1996). Customer contributions to quality: A different view of the customer-oriented firm. *Academy of Management Review, 21,* 791-824.

Lepak, D. P., & Snell, S. A. (1999). The human resource architecture: Toward a theory of human capital allocation and development. *The Academy of Management Review, 24,* 31–48.

Lewin, K. (1951). Problems of research in social psychology. In D. Cartwright (Ed.), *Field theory in social science* (pp. 155–169). New York: Harper & Row.

London House. (1994). *Personnel selection inventory information guide.* Rosemont, IL: Author.

Looy, B. V., Dierdonck, R. V., & Gemmel, P. (Eds.). (1998). *Services management: An integrated approach.* London, England: Financial Times Management.

Lovelock, C. H. (1983). Classifying services to gain strategic marketing insights. *Journal of Marketing, 47,* 9–20.

Lovelock, C. H. (2000). Functional integration in service: Understanding the links between marketing, operations, and human resources. In T. A. Swartz & D. Iacobucci (Eds.), *Handbook of services marketing and management* (pp. 421–437). Thousand Oaks, CA: Sage.

Lovelock, C. H. (2001). *Services marketing: People, technology, strategy* (4th ed.). Englewood Cliffs, NJ: Prentice Hall.

Loveman, G. W. (1998). Employee satisfaction, customer loyalty, and financial performance: An empirical examination of the service profit chain in retail banking. *Journal of Service Research, 1*(1), 18–31.

McGregor, D. M. (1960). *The human side of enterprise.* New York: McGraw-Hill.

Mills, P. K. (1986). *Managing service industries.* Cambridge, MA: Ballinger.

Mills, P. K., Chase, R. B., & Margulies, N. (1983). Motivating the client/employee system as a service production strategy. *Academy of Management Review, 8,* 301–310.

Mills, P. K., & Margulies, N. (1980). Toward a core typology of service organizations. *Academy of Management Review, 5,* 255–265.

Mills, P. K., & Moberg, D. (1982). Perspectives of the technology of service operations. *Academy of Management Review, 7,* 467–478.

Parkington, J. J., & Schneider, B. (1979). Some correlates of experienced job stress: A boundary role study. *Academy of Management Journal, 22,* 270–281.

Rogelberg, S. G., Barnes-Farrell, J. L., & Creamer, V. (1999). Customer service behavior: The inter-action of service predisposition and job characteristics. *Journal of Business and Psychology, 13,* 421–435.

Rogg, K. L., Schmidt, D. B., Shull, C., & Schmitt, N. (2001). Human resource practices, organiza-tional climate, and customer satisfaction. *Journal of Management, 27,* 431–449.

Rucci, A. J., Kim, S. P., & Quinn, R. T. (1998). The employee-customer profit chain at Sears. *Harvard Business Review, 76,* 105–111.

Rust, R. T., Zahorik, A. J., & Keiningham, T. L. (1996). *Service marketing.* New York: HarperCollins.

Schmenner, R. W. (1986). How can service businesses survive and prosper? *Sloan Management Review, 27*(3), 21–32.

Schneider, B. (1994). HRM—A service perspective: Towards a customer-focused HRM. *International Journal of Service Industry Management, 5,* 64–76.

Schneider, B., & Bowen, D. E. (1995). *Winning the service game.* Boston, MA: Harvard Business School Press.

Schneider, B., Bowen, D. E., Ehrhart, M., & Holcombe, K. (2000). The climate for service: Evolution of a construct. In N. M. Ashkanasy, C. P. M. Wilderom, & M. F. Peterson (Eds.), *Handbook of organizational culture and climate* (pp. 21–36). Thousand Oaks, CA: Sage.

Schneider, B., Ehrhart, M. G., Mayer, D., & Saltz, J. (2002). *From personality to profits: A framework for understanding multi-level issues in a service setting.* Working paper, Department of Psychology, University of Maryland.

Schneider, B., Parkington, J. J., & Buxton, V. M. (1980). Employee and customer perceptions of service in banks. *Administrative Sciences Quarterly, 25,* 252–267.

Schneider, B., White, S. S., & Paul, M. C. (1998). Linking service climate and customer perceptions of service quality in banks: Test of a causal model. *Journal of Applied Psychology, 83*(2), 150–163.

Schuler, R. S. (1996). Market-focused management: Human resource management implications. *Journal of Market-Focused Management, 1,* 13–29.

Silvestro, R., & Cross, S. (2000). Applying the service profit chain in a retail environment: Challenging the "satisfaction mirror." *International Journal of Service Industry Management, 11,* 244–268.

Stevenson, W. J. (2002). *Operations management* (7th ed.). New York: McGraw-Hill.

Sutton, R. I., & Rafaeli, A. (1988). Untangling the relationship between displayed emotions and organizational sales: The case of convenience stores. *Academy of Management Journal, 31*(3), 461–487.

Thompson, J. D. (1967). *Organizations in action.* New York: McGraw-Hill.

Verma, R. (1997). An empirical analysis of management challenges in service factories, service shops, and mass services and professional services. *International Journal of Service Industry Management, 11,* 8–25.

Weatherly, K. A., & Tansik, D. A. (1993). Managing multiple demands: A role theory examination of the behaviors of customer contact workers. In T. A. Schwartz, D. E. Bowen, & S. W. Brown (Eds.), *Advances in services marketing and management* (Vol. 2, pp. 253–278). Greenwich, CT: JAI.

Woodward, J. (1965). *Industrial organization: Theory and practice.* Oxford, England: Oxford University Press.

Wright, P. M., Smart, D. L., & McMahan, G. C. (1995). Matches between human resources and strategy among NCAA basketball teams. *Academy of Management Journal, 38,* 1052–1074.

Yoon, M. H., Beatty, S. E., & Suh, J. (2001). The effect of work climate on critical employee behavior and customer outcomes: An employee-level analysis. *International Journal of Service Industry Management, 12,* 500–521.

Youndt, M. A., Snell, S. A., Dean, J. W., Jr., & Lepak, D. P. (1996). Human resource management, manufacturing strategy, and firm performance. *Academy of Management Journal, 39,* 836–866.

Zeithaml, V. A., & Bitner, M. J. (2000). *Services marketing: Integrating customer focus across the firm* (2nd ed.). Boston, MA: McGraw-Hill.

Author Index

Subject Index

About the Authors

Benjamin Schneider is Professor of Psychology at the University of Maryland and a Senior Research Fellow with Personnel Research Associates, Inc. He holds the Ph.D. in Psychology (University of Maryland, 1967) and the M.B.A. (City University of New York, 1964). For 20 years, Dr. Schneider was the head of the Industrial and Organizational Psychology (I-O) program at Maryland. In addition to Maryland, he has taught at Michigan State University and Yale University and, for shorter periods of time, at Dartmouth College's Tuck School of Business Administration, Bar-Ilan University (Israel), University of Aix-Marseilles (France), and Peking University (PRC).

Dr. Schneider's academic accomplishments include more than 90 professional journal articles and book chapters, as well as seven books. His interests concern service quality, organizational climate and culture, staffing issues, and the role of personality in organizational life. He is listed in *Who's Who in America* and derivative volumes, and was awarded the Year 2000 Distinguished Scientific Contributions Award by the Society for Industrial and Organizational Psychology. In addition to his academic work, Dr. Schneider over the years has consulted with numerous companies, including Chase-Manhattan Bank, Citicorp, AT&T, Allstate, Sotheby's, the Metropolitan Opera, Prudential, the states of Alabama and Pennsylvania, GEICO, IBM, American Express, and Giant Eagle.

Susan S. White is a research scientist with the Washington, D.C., office of Personnel Decisions Research Institutes, Inc. She received her M. A. (1998) and Ph.D. (2000) in Industrial and Organizational Psychology from the University of Maryland, and her B.A. in Psychology and Mathematical Economic Analysis (Rice University, 1994). Dr. White's current work focuses primarily on the design and implementation of human resources systems in organizations, including selection, performance management, and training programs. She has worked extensively also in the area of service climate and service quality, and has published her work on these topics in the *Journal of Applied Psychology* and the *Journal of Service Research.*